New Jersey's
Coastal Heritage

New Jersey's Coastal Heritage

A Guide

Mark Di Ionno

RUTGERS UNIVERSITY PRESS
NEW BRUNSWICK, NEW JERSEY

Library of Congress Cataloging-in-Publication Data

Di Ionno, Mark.
    New Jersey's coastal heritage : a guide / Mark Di Ionno.
        p.   cm.
    Includes index.
        ISBN 0-8135-2341-9 (alk. paper). — ISBN 0-8135-2342-7 (pbk. :
    alk. paper)
        1. Atlantic Coast (N.J.)—Guidebooks.   2. New Jersey—
    Guidebooks. I. Title.
        F142.A79D5 1997
        917.49'0443—dc20   96-26025
                                                                CIP

British Cataloging-in-Publication information available

TEXT DESIGN:
    Judith Martin Waterman of Martin-Waterman Associates, Ltd.

Manufactured in the United States of America

For my grandmother, Angelina (Brienza) Tricarico,
whose love and kindness and care made
my Spring Lake days
the best of my life

CONTENTS

Maps and Illustrations

All of the maps have been prepared by Peter Ambush

ACKNOWLEDGMENTS

I would first like to thank Marilyn Campbell and Karen Reeds of Rutgers University Press for approaching me with this project and for their guidance along the way.

Thanks to former *Star-Ledger* editor Mort Pye for giving me the go-ahead to write this book and his successor, Jim Willse, for allowing me to continue. Former Sunday "Accent Page" editor Linda Fowler gets an assist on this project: she assigned me to write the original "Coastal Heritage Trail" story that got the attention of the Rutgers Press editors. Fellow *Star-Ledger* feature writer Bill Gordon, our best historian, furnished some leads and background information on a number of the sites in this book.

Without the expertise of *Star-Ledger* computer whiz Bob Himmelman, this manuscript would probably be bouncing around somewhere in cyberspace, unable to be retrieved by mission control. *Star-Ledger* artist Peter Ambush, illustrator extraordinaire, gave up valuable drawing time to make the maps for this book.

Charles Cummings of the Newark Public Library is responsible for finding most of the historic photos in this book, drawn from the library's collection of seven hundred thousand New

Jersey pictures. Thanks to New Jersey News Photos owner Don Davidson for allowing me to reprint *Star-Ledger* photos, and to News Photos photographer Richard Krauss, my traveling buddy for the *Star-Ledger* series "Postcards from the Jersey Shore" and a good source of shore lore.

Thanks to my brother, John, who accompanied me on a number of barnstorming site trips. (We could drive three hundred miles a day, and he would still be steady enough to take some of the photographs used here.) Thanks to part-time research assistants, Anthony, Michelle, Stephanie, and Matthew Di Ionno, for their honest evaluation of a number of sites. ("Dad, this is boring!" "Be quiet, you might learn something!")

A double thanks to all the people quoted in this book. They added the local color which makes this book different from most tour guides. Thanks, too, to Mr. Jack Jeandron of Steamboat Dock Museum, who graciously gave me a tour of the museum during off hours, Ruth Jackson of Greenwich for spending the good part of a summer afternoon showing me the town; and to Salem County purchaser Curtis Harker for giving me a number of good leads in his area. Sandy Hook historian Thomas Hoffman of the National Park Service and Twin Lights curator Tom Laverty were more than helpful in furnishing information and photos, as were Bob Bright, Jr., of the Boyers Museum in Wildwood; Miles Tourison of the Cape May Historical Society; and Claire Ecker of the Barnegat Light Historical Society. The Trail Manager of the New Jersey Coastal Heritage Trail Route, Philip Correll, was also helpful in furnishing leads and information.

The biggest thanks of all goes to my wife Sharon, who generously afforded me the time to research and write this book. I will return your lost weekends.

*New Jersey's
Coastal Heritage*

INTRODUCTION

The Jersey Shore. For most people it means fun and sun, sand and surf, and hours spent sitting in bumper-to-bumper traffic on the Garden State Parkway.

The Shore is a summer place, opening on Memorial Day, closing after Labor Day, boarded up against the cold and damp months of the New Jersey fall, winter, and spring.

For me, the Shore is where my mother's family has lived for more than a century, first brought to Spring Lake in the early 1890s by her great uncle Ralph Caggiano of Potenza, Italy. Through a relative in Hoboken, seventeen-year-old Ralph Caggiano got word there was work to be had on the Jersey Central Railroad, which was extending train service in the shore area. He jumped the train south and found the work as advertised, laying and maintaining tracks. He then called for his younger brothers, Rocky and Joseph, who came separately over the next six years. For extra money, the brothers took the job of lighting the kerosene street lamps around town in the evening and extinguishing them at dawn. The also worked as laborers on St. Catherine's Church, the elegant cathedral by the town lake.

More relatives followed (my grandparents Paul and Angelina

Tricarico arrived in 1921), and the big immigrant family bought land, built houses, and farmed in the western part of the town, all within two blocks of the train tracks that today form the border between Spring Lake and Spring Lake Heights.

Sixty years and three generations later, I was born in Spring Lake under the most un-summerlike conditions. The day was December 22, 1956, that year's winter solstice and the first full day of winter. A dense, gloomy fog locked over the area, making the darkest day of the year even darker. Perhaps that is why my favorite time to walk the boardwalk is at dusk, particularly on a misty day.

My father and mother moved us away from the shore the following year, inland and north to Summit, New Jersey, but close enough to return at least once a month. Growing up, I did not see the shore as a vacation place, but a place where our grandparents, aunts and uncles, and cousins lived, worked, and went to school. It was a place where we spent Thanksgiving, Christmas, Easter, and winter vacations, as well as summer.

I learned to love the winter desolation at the shore. The words *quiet* and *empty* took on amplified dimensions.

Spring Lake's grand hotels—the Monmouth, the Essex and Sussex, and Warren—would be boarded up, dark, and silent. On summer evenings the sounds of piano music, laughter, and pleasant conversation would float down from their front porches. From the great dining rooms would come the sounds of dinner being served; glasses clinking, the clatter of silverware on fine china. These were the sounds of the affluent living the good life. From the boardwalk, especially on hazy nights, the hotels looked like giant luxury ocean liners, cutting through the darkness, all lit up and festive.

But in winter, the only sound coming from the grand hotels would be the rattling of the plywood on the facades facing the ocean. Against the falling light of winter evenings, their enormous empty hulks would black out huge portions of the gray and orange western sky. In those moments, they looked like ghost ships . . . the landlocked cousins of the *Morro Castle,* which burned within view of the balconies, the *Titanic,* and the *Lusitania.*

In winter, when the boardwalk and beach are deserted, one's thoughts can expand to fill the empty spaces; with the curtain of summer humidity lifted, the horizon is extended. Ships, balanced on the distant line where sea meets sky, go about their business silently, their movement indiscernible to the eye. The only sounds you hear are truly the sounds of nature: the crash of the waves, the squawk of the gulls, the wind combing the dune grass. It is a beautiful season at the beach, if you're sturdy enough to weather it. In winter, the sea can be rougher, the winds more fierce. A simple walk along the water's edge can be a naked challenge to the elements. Need some invigoration? Try a mid-February jaunt down the boardwalk.

Of course, appreciating the merits of peace and quiet is unique to adults.

When I was a kid, nothing beat summer in Spring Lake. We played baseball at the grammar-school field, fished in the lake, and played in my grandmother's backyard, dodging her fruit and fig trees and grapevine trellis. The flat, wide streets were perfect for bicycle riding and the lake, with two wooden foot bridges that span its narrow points, a playground, and tennis courts, was the perfect destination. For one thing, it always seemed ten degrees cooler there than at the beach, and there was a heck of a lot more shade. Also, hanging around the lake put you in striking distance of downtown and the classic 5 & 10 where even the most meager allowance could be stretched to cover a variety of cheap toys and gadgets. There was a little luncheonette called Jerry's, where candy, ice cream, and soda were sold.

Going to the beach was always an option, but rarely the top priority. While most of my girl cousins stayed on the beach from sunup to sundown, my boy cousins couldn't have cared less. My cousin Joe Tricarico spent a couple of college summers working as an auxiliary policeman on the boardwalk. That was the closest he got to the ocean throughout his teen years and into his thirties. Now he goes reluctantly, only to take his baby girl. His brothers, Jerry and Steven, were also beach-haters, opting instead for lake-fishing and baseball. Their father, my uncle Jerry Tricarico, may hold some kind of record for beach avoidance. Although he has spent his entire life living five blocks from the ocean, he hasn't been to the beach to swim or sunbathe in over sixty years. Like almost everyone else in town, he ran down to the beach in the early morning hours of September 8, 1934, as the luxury liner *Morro Castle* was burning offshore.

In recalling the disaster . . . how the fiery ship set the storm-darkened skies aglow off the coast . . . how its passengers staggered out of the surf after swimming ashore . . . how neighbors like the teen-aged Stanley Truax waded into the wicked surf to pull in exhausted survivors . . . how volunteers went door-to-door searching for every available blanket . . . my uncle thought for a moment and said, "I think that was the last time at the beach!"

With year-round access to Spring Lake, I grew up not seeing the shore as a 127-mile-long summer place, but as a series of little homey towns. To me, these towns were not resort towns to be used for three months and forgotten for nine. They were places with yearlong—make that lifelong—continuity. They were great small towns, intimate and warm and friendly. They were places with a history and, in many cases, a maritime legacy. They were places where people put down roots against the ever shifting sands.

Long before the amusement piers, the miniature-golf courses, junk food concession stands, and blocks of motels, the shore towns were places where people went to relax and meditate; places of peace where one's problems seemed insignificant in the face of the most powerful natural force on earth, a sea that could be violent and dangerous, or calm and comforting, depending on its mood.

There is, in all of us, a natural, almost gravitational pull to go there; to feel small against the wide, unobstructed horizon. We look over the ocean and think about the relentless swells, mysterious depths, the creatures below, and the men who challenged them all. The never-ending sky holds the same mysteries and challenges. Air, land, and sea. Galileo and Columbus. It is a magical juncture; the first frontier of man's inherent desire for knowledge, a fertile ground for his unlimited imagination.

This gravitational pull works on me constantly.

There is beauty here; history, too. The iron ore in these hills played an important role in the history (and wars) of this country. George Washington rode along these ridges. The Morris Canal went through here.

There is enough here to make it an adequate adopted home. But my real home, the place that lives inside me, is Spring Lake. I know it is just a matter of time until I return.

For nearly two centuries before the first hotel was built along the Jersey Shore, European settlers and colonists were drawn to the waterfront.

Cape May, which earned National Historic Landmark status based on its reputation as the nation's first resort, was inhabited by whalers, fishermen, sea merchants, and farmers from the time of the first Dutch claim in 1616 until after the War of 1812, when it began to flourish as a resort.

As late as the 1880s, much of Jersey's Atlantic coastline was desolate. Lucy the Margate Elephant, that odd and venerable shore landmark, was basically built as a publicity stunt by a realtor in 1881 to lure investors to the barren oceanfront. The boom in seaside real estate, fueled by the explosion of recreational use of the shore in this century, has overshadowed much of New Jersey's earlier coastal heritage.

"The Shore" is often thought of as one gigantic tourist-attraction entity. In fact, each town has its own culture, identity, and history. The people of Keyport, for instance, share as much in common with the people of Atlantic City, as, say, the people in rural Montague, on the upper reaches of the Delaware River in Sussex County, share with Trentonians. That is to say, not much.

Thankfully, pockets of history have been preserved through the diligence of community historical groups and like-minded individuals. Also, efforts to preserve natural habitats for wildlife have been equally insistent by both private and government concerns.

Until recently, travelers to the shore area would stumble upon these historical and natural attractions by accident. Sure, the history buffs and the bird-watchers knew where to go. But there was no strong, concerted effort to extend tourism beyond beach and boardwalk, to reach the walkabout vacationer whose interests lie beyond what number sunblock to use.

In 1988 federal legislation was passed to create the New Jersey Coastal Heritage Trail. The bill, introduced by then–New Jersey senator Bill Bradley, called for the U.S. Department of the Interior to develop the trail through the National Park Service. The trail is not a specific route, as is the Appalachian Trail, but an immense geographic area along the Atlantic and Delaware Bay sides of New Jersey.

The most significant part of the bill was its definition of "Coastal." The Jersey Shore, by popular definition, has always included the oceanfront and baysides along the Atlantic, from Perth Amboy to Cape May. Long ignored by this definition (and by scads of tourists) was New Jersey's other coast, along the Delaware Bay. With a long history of ship-building and shellfish-harvesting, the Delaware Bay region has as rich a maritime heritage as its neighbor to the east. And yet, it remains a mystery to most shore travelers.

The New Jersey Coastal Heritage Trail is outlined by two major roads: New Jersey State Highway 49, which runs from Pennsville sixty miles east to Tuckahoe, and the 127-mile stretch of the Garden State Parkway from Perth Amboy down to Cape May. The trail area is loosely defined as everything south of Route 49 and everything east of the Parkway. There are a number of exceptions, most notably the twenty-mile area along the Great Egg Harbor River, which begins, inland, northwest of Mays Landing and empties into Great Egg Harbor. The trail is divided into five geographic regions: The Sandy Hook Region, the Barnegat Bay Region, the Cape May Region, the Delsea Region, and the Absecon Region. Sites along the Trail are grouped according to five themes: historic settlements, recreation and inspiration, coastal habitats, wildlife migration, and maritime history. The maritime history theme was the first to be developed; it opened with twenty-eight sites in the fall of 1993, and others have been added since.

Signs for the trail began to spring up on major highways and backroads, directing travelers to coastal heritage sites. By the time the trail is complete, these signs will be familiar landmarks along the coast, marking the sites where wildlife thrives and history lives.

This book is inspired by the New Jersey Coastal Heritage Trail, but has only a loose connection to it. I include many places that have been designated as sites on the Trail, but I have also roved beyond these to highlight a host of other wonderful museums, buildings, byways, and landmarks that could not be incorporated into the official Trail.

The book is organized by county, and each site I describe is located on the county map that opens each section. Every entry gives directions and information about hours, addresses, telephone numbers, and programs, as well as a description of what makes the site special. Although I made every effort to check the accuracy of this information before this book went to press, it is wise to call ahead and make sure that a particular place is open at the time you want to visit.

Now, come with me to these wonderful places where Dutchmen came to hunt whales, where sea captains sailed the coast, where lightkeepers lit the way, where boat-builders kept the fleet afloat, where entrepreneurs built cites for fun, where ministers build cities of faith, and, yes, where my immigrant forebears helped build the railroads.

Monmouth County

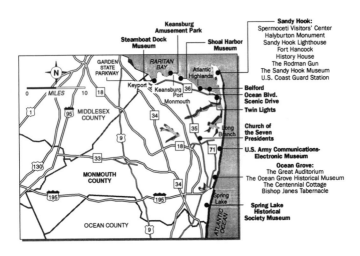

Steamboat Dock Museum

Keansburg Amusement Park

Shoal Harbor Museum

Sandy Hook:
Spermoceti Visitors' Center
Halyburton Monument
Sandy Hook Lighthouse
Fort Hancock
History House
The Rodman Gun
The Sandy Hook Museum
U.S. Coast Guard Station

GARDEN STATE PARKWAY

RARITAN BAY

N

0 MILES 10

18

Atlantic Highlands

Keyport

Keansburg
Port Monmouth

36

Belford

Ocean Blvd. Scenic Drive

Twin Lights

1

95

MIDDLESEX COUNTY

9

34

35

Long Branch

Church of the Seven Presidents

18

71

U.S. Army Communications-Electronic Museum

33

130

MONMOUTH COUNTY

195

34

Ocean Grove:
The Great Auditorium
The Ocean Grove Historical Museum
The Centennial Cottage
Bishop Janes Tabernacle

195

Spring Lake

Spring Lake Historical Society Museum

OCEAN COUNTY

9

ATLANTIC OCEAN

MONMOUTH COUNTY is where the New Jersey's northernmost Atlantic Coast begins, but the county's maritime traditions encompass more than the ocean. The Raritan Bay continues to be home to commercial fishing fleets and recreational marinas, as well as popular beaches. The Sandy Hook Bay attracts the recreational fisherman from sunup to sundown, nine months a year. The Navesink and Shrewsbury rivers are prized sailing spots. If it's big boats you're looking for, then all you need is a pair of binoculars to get right alongside the big freighters and tankers that come in and out of New York Harbor on shipping lanes that run parallel to the Monmouth coast. And anyone who has ever boarded a charter or "party" fishing boat out of Belmar or Brielle knows about the offshore wrecks, favorite feeding spots for fish. With such strong links to the sea, it's hard to believe that Monmouth is also one of the agricultural belts of the state. Orchards thrive in the Colts Neck–Freehold area. Vegetable farms, while shrinking in number, can be found throughout Wall Township, out in Farmingdale, and throughout western Monmouth County in the Allentown area.

This is also horse country. The Cream Ridge is known as Lexington of Standardbred racing. The top thoroughbreds may come from Kentucky, but the best trotters and pacers are the Garden Staters. Monmouth has its share of nonmaritime-related history, too. The Battle of Monmouth was a milestone in the American Revolution, marking the first time American troops held their own against the highly trained British in open field warfare. The battle also gave rise to the legend of Molly Pitcher, who is said to have brought water to thirsty soldiers in the battle and later took her husband's place, firing a cannon when he was injured in battle.

The Steamboat Dock Museum

American Legion Drive
Keyport
(908) 739-6390

OPEN: April and May, Mondays: 10 A.M. to 1 P.M.; June through September, Mondays: 10 A.M. to 1 P.M. and Sundays: 1 P.M. to 4 P.M.; October and November, Mondays: 10 A.M. to 1 P.M. The museum can also be seen by appointment. Call (908) 264-6119, (908) 264-2102, or (908) 264-7822.

COST: Free. Donations welcomed.

DIRECTIONS: Take the Garden State Parkway to Exit 117, to Route 36 east. Follow signs for Keyport. Take Broad Street through town down to waterfront. The museum is at end of Broad, where it turns into American Legion Drive.

By land, sea, or air, the people of the small town of Keyport, on the Raritan Bay, have always found a way to make ends meet. The town actually began as a plantation run by the Kearney family from 1714 until 1829. With seventy slaves and other hired labor, the Kearneys grew produce and produced lumber and had two sloops docked in the bay to transport their goods to New York. The official town of Keyport was formed in 1830 and became a major shipping port (hence, the name) for Monmouth County farmers, millers, and tradesmen. Later in the century Keyport became a steamboat building center and dock area. As transportation technology changed, so did Keyport, and amphibious airplanes were built there from 1917 until the '30s.

The Steamboat Dock Museum has exhibits on all three facets of Keyport history and more. "The Birthplace of Flying Boats" exhibit has a wing from an amphibious plane, pictures of Charles Lindbergh in the cockpit of one of the Keyport-made planes, models of the land-and-sea aircraft, and other artifacts. Most interesting is a photograph of the Uppercu-Burnelli Aircraft Corporation's *Flying Wing*, a giant sea plane with a tiny grill and a massive wing span. Unlike Howard Hughes's wooden *Spruce Goose*, this one got off the ground.

"This plane was ahead of its time because most of the fuel was stored in the wings," said Keyport historian Jack Jeandron.

About fifty steamboats were built in Keyport. One of the first was the *River Queen*, which was used by Gen. Ulysses S. Grant as a dispatch boat in the Potomac River during the Civil War. The *River Queen* hosted Abraham Lincoln on at least one occasion. Other big-name boats built in Keyport were the *Keyport*, of which there is a model, and the *Jesse Hoyt*. Displays have photos of steamboats being built, launched, and underway, and other artifacts. Steamboats docked at Keyport until 1950, when a hurricane around Thanksgiving, battered the coast, wrecked the docks, and deposited the remaining steamboats in people's backyards. Aerial photos of the scene show the boats littered around land, tossed like model ships in a child's sandbox. Other photos, and a *New York Daily News* front page, show the steamboats washed up and wrecked next to beachfront homes, which were equally battered by the storm.

Another bay-related exhibit features the Chingarora Oyster, a slimy delicacy that can only be found in the Keyport area. The Exhibit shows oystermen's tools and gear and features written material on the chingarora, which was so renown among oyster connoisseurs that it was shipped, on ice, out of Keyport to western states, and even to Europe, to meet the demand.

The building that houses the Steamboat Dock Museum was owned by William Gehlhaus, who developed the bayfront of

Keansburg and built the state's first amusement park there (see Keansburg Amusement Park). Gehlhaus's boats ran between New York and Keansburg, but the building that now houses the museum was used as a machine shop and ticket office.

Like many towns along the Raritan Bay, Keyport offers great views of the bay and the connected New York Harbor. From the Steamboat Dock Museum's front door, you can see the Outerbridge Crossing, which connects New Jersey and Staten Island. On a reasonably clear day, you can see the Verrazano-Narrows Bridge and the skyline of lower Manhattan and Brooklyn.

Keansburg Amusement Park

Beachway
Keansburg
(908) 495-1400

OPEN: Summer hours are basically from 9 A.M. to after MIDNIGHT, seven days a week, although many game concessions and rides for older children don't get underway until mid-morning. The park is open seven days a week from late spring until early fall, depending on the weather, and on weekends only, at the very beginning and tail end of the season. For off-season visits, the best bet is to call.

COST: No entrance fee. Rides, games and other attractions vary.

DIRECTIONS: Take the Garden State Parkway to Exit 117, to Route 36 east. Go 5½ miles and look for signs for Keansburg Amusement Park. Take either Main Street or Laurel 1½ miles north of Route 36 to Beachway.

The Keansburg Amusement Park is the oldest in New Jersey and one of the first thirty built in the country.

The park was built by William A. Gehlhaus, a baker and real-estate developer, who also built the Keanburg beachfront.

Just after the turn of the century, his company, the New Point Comfort Beach Company, pumped sand from the bottom of the Raritan Bay to make the marshy coastline along the bay inhabitable. Streets were laid out, lots for seaside bungalows were sold. A mile-long bulkhead was constructed to keep the new land intact, and the boardwalk built behind it. Gehlhaus opened the Keansburg Amusement Park in 1904.

Gehlhaus's son, Henry, sold the park in 1972, but his sons, William and Hank, bought it back in 1994 to continue the family tradition.

Hank, a ride operator and concessionaire at the park for twenty years, knew the brothers had to move quickly when the former owners began to think of selling.

"We both realized this was the time to do something. We realized that in our life span, it might not change hands again. This has always been a family operation."

"Our family just took a twenty-two-year vacation from this business," is the way William, a local attorney, explains it. "Now we're back, getting bigger and better, with every intention of becoming more family oriented than ever."

So the Gehlhaus's family tradition continues, and if there's one thing The Keansburg Amusement Park is, it's traditional.

Unlike most amusement parks that struggle to keep up with the latest amusement technology or faddish commercial themes, Keansburg has that vintage feel. Like a '50s teenager who kept his flat-top crew-cut through adulthood only to find it back in style in the '90s, Keansburg Amusement Park seems unflappable in its classic approach to boardwalk entertainment. Fans of the long gone North Jersey amusement parks, Palisades and Olympic, will love this place. It is small, friendly, and clean. The roller coaster and main Ferris wheel, as well as the tilt-a-wheel and Himalayan ride are oldies, but goodies. The prices are vintage, too. Some arcade games can be played for a quarter, or even a dime. A 110-ticket ride book goes for $30, about 27-cents a ticket, and most rides cost between three and five tickets. It's boardwalk amusement at church fair prices. The 6½-acre park has 42 rides with enough kiddie selections to keep a family with toddlers occupied all day.

If you need a break from the carnival atmosphere, there are nine and a half acres of dunes and beach adjacent to the park and a twenty-four hundred-foot fishing pier.

Street parking is limited (meters take a quarter for 30 minutes), but the park parking lot has adequate space for the weekend crowd. The park offers fireworks displays throughout the summer on special nights. Call for information.

The Shoal Harbor Museum
(also known as **The Spy House**)

119 Port Monmouth Road.
(908) 787-1807

OPEN: Saturdays and Sundays: 2 P.M. to 4 P.M. Group tours can be arranged by calling the museum.

COST: Free. Donations accepted.

DIRECTIONS: Take the Garden State Parkway to Exit 117, to Route 36 east. Follow signs to Port Monmouth. Take Main Street until it crosses Wilson and bear left on Wilson. Spy House is at the end of Wilson.

There is a new trend at the Shoal Harbor Museum, formerly known as the Spy House. The volunteers and board members of the museum want to accentuate the history rather than legend. Unfortunately, so much legend has surrounded the white clapboard and green shuttered colonial rambler that overlooks the Sandy Hook Bay, that the history seems tame by comparison.

First the legend.

The house was given the name Spy House by a British officer who picked up on the following trend. Each time British officers and sailors would leave their ships to come to the Spy House, which, in those days, was supposedly an inn, their ships would be attacked by patriots in whaleboats.

More legend.

The house is said to be haunted by no less than thirty spirits, one of which inhabits a broken, blonde-haired mannequin that sits in a rocking chair in an upstairs bedroom. There have been a number of claimed spirit sightings at the house over the years. A sobbing woman named Abigail, apparently gazing out to sea for a husband who will never return, frequents an upstairs window. A young boy, presumed to be her son, Peter, is sometimes seen with her and other times seen running amok through the house. A black-hooded, evil sea captain, said to have been a devil-worshiper in life, prowls the grounds in eternal penance.

Now for the history.

Part of the house was originally built by Thomas Whitlock, a itinerant English carpenter in 1663. The house was then sold to Daniel Seabrook, the patriarch of the farming family that would eventually make a fortune in frozen foods in the early 1900s. (Seabrook Farms is in business today, in the Vineland area.) Daniel Seabrook developed the acreage around him as farmland, growing fruit trees, raising livestock, farming vegetables. Before long, Seabrook had one of the biggest plantations in the area.

The house stayed in the Seabrook family for generations. Another owner, Reverend William Wilson, was the principal owner of a profitable steamboat company in the area. (More legend: psychics sense Rev. Wilson leading funeral services in front of a bedroom fireplace, and the ghost in the mannequin is believed to be his wife.)

"The folklore was a lot of fun, but many of those things were conjured up," said Peg Corcoran, a volunteer at the museum. "We felt that the house itself, and it's history, were not being addressed. They were being lost."

Corcoran admits there seems to be "a high level of energy" in the house, but that the ghost stories have been overblown.

"It got to a point where people would come, and that's all they would want to know about," she said. "It's best to leave those things for people who are interested in it. For other people, it scares them."

The house serves as a catch-all museum for the Shoal Harbor and Port Monmouth area. Only two pieces of furniture are documented as having been part of the home: a bed belonging to one of the Seabrooks that had been moved away and then donated back and a bookcase built by Rev. Wilson. But there are other pieces that date back to the 1700s, including spinning wheels, farm tools, fishing tools for eeling and crabbing, fishing nets, and a few whalebones.

"We're trying to promote the three hundred years of history in the house, so we have a few things from every period, including this century," Corcoran said.

The grounds around the house are open to the public even when the museum is closed. There are picnic benches protected by shade and an eclectic collection of outdoor exhibits, including lobster traps, antique farm equipment, anchors, mechanical and hand pumps, and a set of stockades. Written on the stockades are some of the crimes that would get an offender a few hours of public humiliation: working on Sundays, spitting, and talking too much (females only).

A walk to the beach right behind the house offers a sweeping view of the Sandy Hook Bay and New York Harbor, including an Oz-like visage of Lower Manhattan.

The museum encourages visitors to call ahead on brutally hot days in the summer. With no air conditioning and poor ventilation, the house becomes too hot for volunteer workers to stand.

Belford Waterfront

End of Main Street
Belford

DIRECTIONS: Take the Garden State Parkway to Exit 117.
Follow Route 36 east, and look for signs to Belford.

For those who think they must go to Cape Cod or
Bar Harbor to see old-time fishing villages, a trip to Belford,
instead, will cut days off your travel time.

But if you're looking for quaintness and charm and crusty
old Popeye-looking characters hanging around the souvenir
wharf, you might as well head to New England. Belford is Jersey grit, a working fisherman's village. In Belford, you see fishing
nets strung out along front lawns, opened for repair. You see
lobsters traps and clam cages stacked in backyards. You see
decaying boats propped up on wood cradles with For Sale signs
fading in the sun. Belford is a fishing town, shaped not by

MARK DI IONNO

The fishing boats and pleasure crafts at the Belford Waterfront.

tourists and fancy seafood restaurants, but by families who, for generations, have sailed out before dawn and back in after dark to harvest fish from the bays and ocean. This is hard work. And between competition from foreign and domestic fishing conglomerates, government regulations, and depleted fish populations, its been virtually impossible for independent fishermen to stay in business.

The dozen or so fishing families of Belford—Egnatovich, Isakson, Schnoor, Richmond, to name a few—formed a co-operative in 1956 as a way to combat the big fishmongers in the New York market who were trying to drive prices down.

In the past forty years, the united-we-stand efforts of the co-op have helped the local fisherman survive.

"This is the oldest fishing port on the East Coast," said Bob Egnatovich, the manager of the co-op and a third-generation member of a four-generation fishing family. "We date back to the Dutch colonists. We have history here we haven't even uncovered yet. It would be a tragedy if we went under."

Egnatovich said the key to success is to get the fish directly to the consumer as fast as possible—and in any amount the customer demands. For that reason the Belford co-op has a wholesale market, a retail store, and a new, casual restaurant.

"My motto is 'I'll sell you forty thousand pounds or a fish sandwich,'" Egnatovich said. "Seafood has gotten to be a luxury item. It used to be that people would eat fish because it was less expensive than meat. Nowadays, there are so many middlemen involved, the price keeps going up and less money goes back to the boat (the fisherman). If we cut out those middlemen, the consumer saves money and more money goes back to the boat."

One reason the Belford co-op has been successful is that the fishing community is tight knit.

"I'd say there are about a dozen families who make up 90 percent of the dock," Egnatovich said. "Fishermen are the most independent people you can meet, but down here they all un-

derstand what we have to do to survive. Even then, it is sometimes hard to get everybody pulling in the same direction, and
co-ops, farming, fishing, whatever, have been going out of business left and right. But we're hanging in there."

The retail outlet is open Monday through Saturday, 8:30
A.M. to 4:30 P.M., and on Sundays from 8:30 A.M. till NOON. The
restaurant, called The Catch of the Day, is open from 11 A.M. to
7 P.M., seven days a week, and offers home delivery, take-out,
and catering, as well as indoor and outdoor dining.

The Views from Ocean Boulevard

Off Route 36
Atlantic Highlands

DIRECTIONS: Take the Garden State Parkway to Exit 117,
Route 36 east to exit for Scenic Road and Mount
Mitchell.

Ocean Boulevard is to New Jersey what the Pacific
Coast Highway is to California. Okay, maybe that's a little
exaggeration. Ocean Boulevard isn't as big a tourist attraction
as the PCH. Not nearly as long, either. And the drops aren't as
dramatic. But for drive-by, bird's-eye views of the shorefront,
it's the best view in New Jersey that isn't manmade. The Boulevard runs about five miles along the Sandy Hook Bay from
the scenic overlook at Mount Mitchell down to the Atlantic
Highlands Municipal Marina, with its Victorian gazebo and
pleasant parkgrounds. Mount Mitchell, being the highest point
on the scenic road, offers the best view along the drive and is
second only to Twin Lights (see Twin Lights State Historic
Site) in the region. At Mount Mitchell there is ample parking
and a few sets of high-powered commercial binoculars so visitors can zero in on an outgoing fishing boat from Belford, or
the Manhattan skyline, or a jet-skier in the Sandy Hook Bay,
or a big barge heading for the Verrazano-Narrows Bridge. From

Mount Mitchell, Ocean Boulevard heads west toward the town center of Atlantic Highlands. There is one lookout spot along the road, across from a German-American restaurant. The road cuts into a bluff that runs parallel to the shoreline. Many of the shore-side homes are tucked into the hillside and do not impede the motorists view of the bay, the hook, and ocean. There are a number of marinas along the Highlands-area coast, so the water is always capped by white sails. If the day is cloudy, you can always enjoy the architectural sites along the Boulevard: the homes range from Frank Lloyd Wright–type geometric moderns to Victorian mansions.

The Boulevard is winding, with descending curves 'round every bend. It is also a favorite stretch for joggers and bicyclists, so enjoy the scenery, but keep one eye on the road. Best advice: obey the 25 MPH speed limit.

Sandy Hook Unit

> Gateway National Recreation Area
> Off Route 36
> East of Atlantic Highlands
> (908) 872-0115

OPEN: Park grounds open sunrise to sunset, every day.

COST: From Memorial weekends and holidays. Admission price gives visitors access to all beaches, museums, nature walks, and historic sites. Before 7 A.M. and after 5 P.M., there is no charge.

DIRECTIONS: Take the Garden State Parkway to Route 36 east. Follow it into Sandy Hook.

Sandy Hook is different things to different people. For nature lovers there are acres of unspoiled dunes and abundant wildlife. For a different sort of "naturalist," there is the only clothing-optional beach on New Jersey's Atlantic Coast. For military buffs there are the remains of Fort Hancock, which has featured everything from the retractable guns at-the-ready during the Spanish-American War, to the nuclear Nike missiles from the heyday of the Cold War. For maritime buffs there is the oldest working lighthouse in the United States and an active Coast Guard Station. Part of the Gateway National Recreation Area that rings New York Harbor, Sandy Hook is indeed the gate to the metropolitan area's coastal waterways. And a swinging gate at that: aerial views of the Hooks from the 1940s show how dramatically sand-shifting and erosion have changed the six-and-a-half-mile sand spit.

The best way to see Sandy Hook is to set aside a day and get information on what museums are open and what tours are available for the day you plan to visit. Federal spending cuts have played havoc with park schedules and one museum, the History House, is staffed solely by volunteers. The main number (908) 872-0115 hooks you into the ranger station. Ask for the Spermaceti Cove Visitors' Center and the National Park Service employee on duty there will have all the information.

Seasonal program guides and schedules are available by writing:

Gateway National Recreation Area Headquarters
Division of Interpretation & Recreation
Floyd Bennett Field
Brooklyn, NY 11234

Ask to be put on the federal park's mailing list and you will receive schedules of activities like gun-battery tours of Fort Hancock, Ranger-led nature walks, museum tours, guided tours of the salt marshes, and summer night prowls of the beaches and trails.

In the meantime, here's a whirlwind tour of The Hook:

The Spermaceti Cove Visitors' Center

OPEN: 10 A.M. to 5 P.M. daily except Thanksgiving, Christmas, and New Years Day. Call (908) 872-0115 for information.

The Spermaceti Cove Visitors' Center, which is the main information station for Sandy Hook, is also a museum with two main exhibits. The first deals with nature, the second with nature's deadly forces.

The natural museum section of the Visitors' Center has everything from tame seashell and driftwood displays, to some wild taxidermy action shots, including a predator owl wringing a ring-necked pheasant by the neck. Other display cases have stuffed gray squirrels and white-footed field mice in their natural habitats, ditto for raccoons and muskrats. There are birds and ducks, too: the common tern, the house sparrow, black ducks, and a great blue heron suspended from the ceiling, in flight for the ages.

The other part of the museum is a new exhibit on the United States Life Saving Service (USLSS), the forerunner to the U.S. Coast Guard. All of the equipment and uniforms on display are reproductions, but interesting just the same. With forty-two stations along the coast, from Sandy Hook to Bayshore at Cape May Point, the Life Saving Service had a presence in almost every town (compare it to the number of local fire departments today.)

The idea behind the USLSS came from Dr. William A. Newell, who watched in horror in August of 1839 as a ship got stuck on a sand bar three hundred yards from shore and broke up as storm waves pounded it; the crew of thirteen slipped into the sea and drowned. It was a spectacle he never wanted to see again, and he dedicated his life to making the seas safer. (Shipwrecks were common along the Jersey Coast for two reasons: first, the treacherous network of shifting sand bars along the barrier islands, bays, and coves made navigation a guess at best; second, the amount of ship traffic off Jersey, being situated between New York and Philadelphia, was extraordinarily heavy.)

As a U.S. Congressman, Newell introduced legislation to appropriate ten thousand dollars for manpower, surfboats, and lifeline equipment, and the United States Life Saving Service was born. (About the same time, Joseph Francis of Toms River was perfecting his lifecar, a one-man metal container that ferried survivors from ship to shore, which became an important component of the USLSS. See the Toms River Seaport Society Museum entry in the Ocean County chapter.)

The USLSS exhibit at Spermaceti Cove has a ten-minute video on the USLSS and a number of original photographs and newspaper accounts of sea rescues. There are also photographs of the original Spermaceti Cove station (now at Twin Lights State House site) and the bigger replacement building built in 1894, which is now the Visitors' Center building.

The equipment on display is a testimony to good, old-fashioned Yankee ingenuity: small cannons that would fire missiles with ropes attached to the ship; the big-wheeled beach cart that would hold the rope much like a horse-drawn fire wagon held hose; the breeches buoy, nothing more than a pair of canvas pants sown into a life preserver. The survivor sat in the breeches and was pulled in on the line.

Also on display are uniforms: two "Surfmen's" winter dress blues and a set of summer whites. Duly noted: the men lobbied Congress for official uniforms, but had to pay for them themselves.

All in all, it's an outstanding exhibit that will hold the interest of adults and fidgety kids alike . . . even on a perfect beach day.

The Halyburton Monument

Right off the main park road, about 2 miles north of the Visitors' Center, is the Halyburton Monument. A British naval officer named Halyburton volunteered to leave the British warship H.M.S. *Assistance* and go ashore to round up a group of deserters in December of 1783. But Halyburton and his search-and-seize party of thirteen men got caught in a fierce New Year's Eve blizzard, capsized, and either drowned or froze to death near Horseshoe Cove.

The men were buried near there, resting in peace until 1908 when the U.S. Army unearthed their bones while digging a railroad bed. A monument was constructed, but was destroyed by vandals. In the 1930s, the Civilian Conservation Corps built the existing monument.

The Sandy Hook Lighthouse

Here's a little-known fact: The Sandy Hook Lighthouse was built with money from the lottery. That's right, two hundred years before New Jersey legalized the numbers racket to nourish the state kitty, the New York Colonial Assembly approved two lotteries to pay for a lighthouse at the tip of Sandy Hook. The governing body was pressed into action by New York merchants, who were sick of seeing ships carrying their merchandise wrecked on the shoals and sandbars around The Hook.

The lighthouse became operational on June 11, 1764. During the Revolution, the lighthouse was an eighty-five-foot pawn in the battle between British loyalists and revolution-minded colonists. Patriots tried to destroy the Tory-controlled lighthouse in an attempt to confuse British warships, and maybe send a few into the sand shoals. The lighthouse survived to become a National Historic Landmark on its bicentennial, and it is the

The Sandy Hook Lighthouse (background) couldn't keep the brig Lady Napier *from grounding on "The Hook" in 1907. Courtesy of Newark Public Library.*

oldest working lighthouse in the nation. It is operated by the U.S. Coast Guard. The inside is closed to the public, but the grounds are open to everyone.

The lighthouse's nonblinking white light can be seen from nineteen miles out at sea, on clear nights. In the daytime, the tower marks the left side of the New York Harbor entrance.

Here's another interesting fact about the changing shape of Sandy Hook. When the lighthouse was built, it was five hundred feet from the northern most tip of The Hook. Now, after two hundred years of current-carried sand deposits, it is one and a half miles from the northern most tip of the sand spit.

Fort Hancock

OPEN: Outdoor gun batteries can always be visited by self-guided tour. Call (908) 872-0115 for guided tour information.

As the gateway to the New York harbor, Sandy Hook always had strategic importance. The fact that it was desolate also made it the perfect spot for military development. Fort

Hancock, one of two concrete gun batteries built in New Jersey at the end of the nineteenth century, was designed to protect the New York Harbor, Fort Mott watched over the Delaware Bay (see Fort Mott in *Salem County*).

The leap in warfare technology made during the American Civil War led a number of European nations to bolster their naval strength. The United States, historically protective of its harbors, moved to reinforce its coastal defenses. Concrete gun batteries served a number of purposes: they could withstand a heavy shelling, they blended in with the natural landscape for camouflage, and they were strong enough to support the big guns that could punch a hole in an enemy warship a few miles out at sea.

The twelve-inch guns at the Sandy Hook Mortar Battery could launch a seven hundred-pound missile. There were sixteen of these guns, clustered in groups of four. Fired simultaneously and on target, it could make an enemy warship would look like it got stuck in a hailstorm of falling safes.

KLAUS SCHNITZER, MONTCLAIR STATE COLLEGE

Klaus Schnitzer's arrangement of old ordnance used at Fort Hancock.

KLAUS SCHNITZER, MONTCLAIR STATE COLLEGE

Photographer Klaus Schnitzer's artistic view of the tunnel at Battery Potter, Sandy Hook.

At Batteries Potter and Granger the emphasis was on stealth warfare. The two, twelve-inch guns at Battery Potter were mounted on a steam-powered elevator. First floor, firing. Basement, loading. The guns could hit a battle ship seven miles at sea with a thousand-pound missile. Potter was completed in 1893. By 1896, the Army had developed counterbalanced, retractable guns. A system of counterweights, allowed the gun crew to raise the heavy artillery into firing position. The gun's recoil, would swing it down below, where it was reloaded out of sight, hence the term disappearing guns.

The guns at Battery Gunnison were smaller, but faster firing guns. They were designed to hit smaller, but faster moving ships.

Sandy Hook was also home to the nation's first proving ground for weapons and ordnance, beginning in 1874. Nearly a century later it housed a number of Nike-missile launchers for Cold War protection. (A missile is displayed at Guardian Park at Fort Hancock). The Nike Ajax, planted at Sandy Hook from 1954 to 1959, could find enemy aircraft within thirty miles and could reach a top altitude of sixty thousand feet. Its successor, the Nike Hercules, had a range of over a hundred miles and could scrape the heavens at one hundred fifty thousand feet. One other thing: the Hercules carried a nuclear bang.

Fort Hancock was officially decommissioned at the end of 1974. The old gun batteries had fallen into disrepair and a number were deemed unsafe and torn down.

History House

OPEN: Saturdays and Sundays: 1 P.M. to 5 P.M.

After passing the two Nike missiles at Guardian Park, visitors to Sandy Hook will pass a row of twenty homes overlooking the Sandy Hook Bay. The last of these is the History House, built as a lieutenant's quarters in 1898. The History House is a small museum with exhibits on domestic life in the Army from 1890 to the 1970s. The house is filled with furniture and appliances from that 80-year time span, as well as photographs and other Army-life artifacts.

The Rodman Gun

Just as the two Nike missiles at Guardian Park document the most recent use of Fort Hancock, the Rodman gun goes back to the earliest days. In fact, the Rodman predates the Fort by about twenty-five years. When the big gun was shipped to Fort Hancock, it was not to take its place among the heavy artillery, but to waste away in a rust heap with other unwanted guns.

The Rodman gun, which is displayed outdoors just north of History House on the Fort Hancock grounds, was invented by Army officer Thomas J. Rodman. It was the biggest of the muzzle-loading, smooth-bore cannons Rodman designed and had cast by

The Rodman gun. Courtesy of Sandy Hook Museum, National Park Service.

his own methods. During the Civil War, Rodman guns, in eight, ten- and fifteen-inch sizes were used. By wars end, Rodman cast a twenty incher, which today sits at Fort Hamilton in Brooklyn. The second twenty incher, which weighed fifty-seven and a half tons, was made in 1869, but was already obsolete. Eventually, it ended up at the Proving Ground graveyard until it was saved and preserved by a Rodman fan, who happened to be the commanding officer of the fort in 1903.

The Sandy Hook Museum

OPEN: Saturdays and Sundays: 1 P.M. to 5 P.M.

This museum has a little of everything: dioramas of Fort Hancock, a collection of some of the shells used there, gun models, and a small display about the lighthouse.

The museum is staffed by volunteers, so it is best to call ahead for schedule information at (908) 872-0115.

United States Coast Guard Station

(908) 872-0326

The Coast Guard base at the northernmost tip of Sandy Hook is not open to the public, but people can gain access by calling the above number to arrange a visit. The Sandy Hook station is small compared to the base at Cape May (see *Cape May County*) which has the recruits' training center and an air wing, including the red helicopters that scour the coast. At Sandy Hook, there are two, one hundred ten-foot cutters and a handful of smaller vessels. The search-and-rescue air support for the region comes out of the Brooklyn base, so there are no planes or helicopters at the Hook.

Twin Lights State Historic Site

Lighthouse Road (off Route 36 east)
Highlands
(908) 872-1814

OPEN: Memorial Day to Labor Day, daily: 10 A.M. to 5 P.M. Off-season hours: Wednesday through Sunday: 10 A.M. to 5 P.M.

COST: Free. Donations accepted.

DIRECTIONS: Take the Garden State Parkway to Exit 117, take Route 36 east. The well-marked exit for Twin Lights is right before the bridge to Sandy Hook. From there, head up, up, up. *The access road is steep and narrow with one blind turn. Be careful!*

From the sea walls of Sea Bright to the bay shores of Sandy Hook, the Twin Lights of the Navesink hover over the landscape, the crown atop the highest bluff of the Highlands. The jewels in the crown no longer shine, but when they did, they could be seen some twenty-two miles out at sea. The twin lighthouses helped countless ships, entering or leaving New

The Twin Lights was a popular picnic grounds at the turn of the century. Twin Lights Historical Society.

York Harbor, navigate the treacherous waters off Sandy Hook. The Twin Lights, 64 feet high, are 246 feet above sea level, sea level being the bottom of the bluff on which the lights stand. That extreme elevation against the flatness of the shoreline gives the Twins Lights such a towering presence.

The height of the bluff made it a natural spot for any type of communications system, be it bonfire or radio antenna. Historians can trace the first beacon there to around 1746, when Colonists used the bluff as part of an early-warning system against enemy forces. If more than five ships were seen convoying into the harbor and were deemed unfriendly, the beacon

A recent view from Twin Lights. Courtesy of The Star-Ledger.

was lit and alarm sounded in New York. The first lighthouse towers went up in 1828, and by 1862, the two brownstone towers that mark the spot today were standing. The first Fresnel lens used in America was at Twin Lights; it was put in the South Tower in 1841. Lens technology improved, and the South Tower got a bivalve lens in 1898 which, coupled with the Twin Lights homegrown electricity (it was the only lighthouse on the coast to have it's own power plant), made Twin Lights the most powerful beacon in the United States.

The power of the South beacon blanched out the North Tower light and it was closed in 1898, except for emergencies. The South Tower light was discontinued in 1952. Of course, the towering structure still serves as a daytime landmark for sailors, pilots, and drivers in the area.

As impressive as the Twin Lights are from below, the view *from* the Twin Lights is stunning. Below are the village-like neighborhoods of Highlands and Sea Bright. Rumson sits on the other side of the Navesink. Boats are everywhere. On the bayside, on the ocean, on the Navesink. Boats of all kinds—

personal watercraft (jet skis), sailboats, pleasure crafts, commercial and party fishing boats, tugboats pulling barges, container ships, and oil tankers on the horizon. Sandy Hook lies to the north like a lean cat stretching out on a blue carpet. To the south is another sand spit, the built up barrier island that holds Sea Bright and Monmouth Beach. You can see the waves spray up over the sea walls, an every-few-seconds reminder that Mother Nature is always knocking at the door.

All this can be seen from the lighthouse grounds, an expanse of yard that stretches from the north side of the lighthouse and all along it's 350-foot front. The view from the North Tower (the South Tower is closed to the public) adds the dimension of height, but it is not a place to linger. It is cramped and hot, very hot. Talk about your greenhouse effect: the plexiglass that surrounds the tower lets the heat in and keeps any breeze out and, since hot air rises, it all just hangs there, waiting to mug unsuspecting tourists. Also: WATCH YOUR HEAD going up the circular stairs. The metal overhangs are well-marked but most people, when climbing unfamiliar stairs, have a tendency

The surf pounding the sea wall at Sea Bright, a good example of the cause of the ever-changing shoreline. Courtesy of Newark Public Library.

to look at their feet rather than straight ahead. A thunk of the forehead against one of those unforgiving metal overpasses may actually enhance the view . . . you'll see double.

The grounds, on the other hand, are breezy and pleasant, and virtually free of head-injury risk. The original Spermaceti Cove (ca. 1849) life-saving station is there, and even though it looks like nothing more than a brown-shingled one-car garage, it's kind of neat to recognize it in photographs from the 1800s on display at the Sandy Hook life-saving exhibit at Spermaceti Cove (see Spermaceti Cove Visitors' Center at Sandy Hook). There is an example of a metal lifecar inside the garage, as well as inside the Twin Lights museum.

Also on the grounds is a memorial to the Marconi Tower, a hundred-foot antenna that was the first to transmit wireless telegraph messages in the United States.

After one visit to Monmouth County, Marconi knew the topography of the area was perfect for ship-to-shore (and later, shore-to-shore) communications. Marconi built the tower at Twin Lights specifically to prove there was a commercial use for wireless radio communication. The first broadcast was on September 30, 1899, from the *Ponce,* which was part of the Commodore George Dewey fleet which drove the Spanish armada from the Philippines. Marconi boarded the *Ponce* as the fleet returned to New York Harbor and dispatched a news story back to Twin Lights. The messages were then sent to a telegraph station in Highlands, then to New York. Marconi's tower operated at Twin Lights until 1907, when he began moving most of his operations to Cape Cod. He did maintain a presence at the Jersey Shore, and built the world's first trans-Atlantic tower in Belmar nearly a decade later. If you follow the twisting Marconi Road four miles off Route 138 in Belmar, you will find a plaque dedicated to the achievement.

Twin Lights State Historic Site curator, Tom Laverty, said the Marconi Tower opened the door to future over-the-air communications.

"This was a big step," Laverty said. "This was the beginning of the use of wireless communication signals. Once Marconi did this, once he showed it could be commercially viable, it led to the proliferation of wireless and radio communication devices."

In other words, the Marconi Tower is the great-great-great grandfather of the modern-day telecommunications satellite.

Inside Twin Lights, there is a museum at the base of the North Tower in the former eighteen-room keeper's quarters. The museum has a little of everything: Marconi, United States Lifesaving Service history, lighthouse technology, and a neat little postcard collection that shows Twin Lights through various artists' and photographers' eyes and angles through the ages. Two exhibits that will grab kids: the cleaning-the-lens case with feather dusters, brushes, and other antiques. The other is the shipwreck display, which includes this banner headline in a 1914 *Long Branch Daily Record*: SEVEN PERISH IN SIGHT OF THOUSANDS HERE AS THREE-MASTED SCHOONER GOES TO PIECES.

Church of the Presidents

> 1260 Ocean Avenue
> Long Branch
> (908) 299-0600

OPEN: By appointment only. Call (908) 299-0600.

COST: Free

DIRECTIONS: Take the Garden State Parkway to Exit 105 and head east on Route 36. Take 36 to Ocean Avenue and head south. The church is in an area of multimillion-dollar mansions and estates and religious retreats, south of the Long Branch public beachfront. Do not confuse the Church of the Presidents with the Seven Presidents County Park, which is at the north end of Long Branch. The county park is strictly recreational, offering a swimming beach and concession stands. There is nothing historical, either in artifacts or in location about it. It is important to note that Route 36 originates in Keyport off Parkway Exit 117, follows the shoreline east along the Raritan Bay, then turns south to follow the shoreline of the Atlantic Ocean. At Long Branch, Route 36 heads west again, hooking up with the Parkway at Exit 105. Confusing? Yes. But it's nothing that a New Jersey map can't clear up. And either way, Route 36 always ends up in Long Branch.

Ulysses S. Grant had the summer White House there. Rutherford B. Hayes and Benjamin Harrison frequented the Elberon Hotel. James A. Garfield spent his last days there, in the hopes that the salt air and cool ocean breezes would help him recover from gunshot wounds.

In all, seven United States presidents visited Long Branch. All seven attended services at St. James Episcopal Church, and Garfield's body was brought there before being shipped to Washington after his death.

The Church of the Presidents is the last reminder of the days when Long Branch attracted the nation's most rich, famous, and powerful. Unfortunately, the famous church is also in danger of slipping into history.

The church, which is headquarters of the Long Branch Historical Society, is structurally unsound in places. Walls are buckling and jacks are being used to hold up the section by the altar. Some of its beautiful stained-glass windows are in jeopardy as the walls sag.

Despite its historical relevance, the Church may not survive the coming decade. Long Branch Historical Society president Edgar N. Dinkelspiel says there doesn't seem to be enough interest about town history among current residents.

"We can't even get enough volunteers to open the museum on a regular basis, let alone find the manpower and money to renovate the church," he said.

The church has received a few grants from time to time and recently applied for a grant from the New Jersey Historic Trust, but the needed work is so extensive Dinkelspiel is not optimistic. "We'll keep it going as long as we can," he said. "After that, who knows?"

There are many examples of historical places going down with the neighborhoods around them (the original Walt Whitman house in Camden fell into disrepair, became vacant, then burned down). Such is not the case with the Church of the Presidents. The church is surrounded by mansions of every architectural style from ultramodern to Mediterranean to Medieval. On the day I visited the church, a neighboring family was out posing for pictures with their new Rolls-Royce. It's a shame the residents there don't have the foresight to realize they are an ongoing part of town legend. It's a shame they don't realize being gone is the first step in being forgotten, and if the church goes, the most important part of Long Branch history goes with it.

Church of the Presidents in Long Branch, shown here in 1985, has deteriorated considerably in the past decade. Courtesy of Newark Public Library.

So much in Long Branch has already gone. The Elberon Hotel; the Hollywood Hotel, where Arthur stayed; the West End Hotel, where Garfield first stayed; and the Francklyn Cottage, where Garfield died, are all gone.

Grant's summer White House, which was at 991 Ocean Avenue, is also gone, knocked down in the early 1960s. The land is now part of the property of the Stella Maris Retreat.

"I tried to contact President Kennedy to try to save it, but all the government did was send people up to take pictures of it the day they knocked it down," Dinkelspiel said.

Dinkelspiel has binders filled with postcards and photographs of old Long Branch, including pictures of the palatial Guggenheim mansions—Solomon, Murray, Randolph and Daniel each had summer homes there—and other giant summer "cottages" of the extremely wealthy. Other artifacts range from a Durnell piano, made by the Durnell Company of Long Branch, to a horse-drawn hose wagon of the Long Branch Fire Department.

On the walls of the church are bronze plaques honoring the six presidents: Woodrow Wilson, the last to visit Long Branch; Grant, who was not only the first president to visit there but who ushered in an era of Long Branch chic; Hayes; Chester Arthur; Garfield; and McKinley, who was assassinated in office twenty years after Garfield's murder. For some reason, there is no plaque commemorating Harrison, a fact that has baffled Long Branch Historical Society members for years.

A bit of macabre trivia: only four U.S. presidents have been assassinated, and three were known to summer at the Jersey Shore. Garfield and McKinley came to Long Branch, while Abraham Lincoln favored Cape May. John F. Kennedy, of course, had Cape Cod.

The current crisis is not the first for the church. It fell into disrepair in the 1930s but was rescued by a group of citizens led by Louis V. Aronson, the Newark inventor and metal artist who made Ronson lighters, and Lewis B. Tim, the wealthy shirt manufacturer. There are bronze plaques in the church commemorating these men, as well as earlier residents Anthony J. Drexel, the Philadelphia banker and financier, and George W. Childs, the publisher of the *Philadelphia Inquirer.*

Also inside is a portrait of Thomas Edison, but it is not known if he ever attended services there. A similar portrait of Grant was stolen.

In its heyday, Long Branch attracted not only presidents and wealthy business men—George Pullman, the inventor of the Pullman car was also a resident—but stage and screen celebrities such as British actress Lillie Langtry, who lived in a private rail car each summer; Oscar Wilde; the Barrymore family; Buffalo Bill and Annie Oakley; and Lillian Russell, often escorted by Diamond Jim Brady in a specially built electric car with a brightly illuminated interior, so everyone on the outside could see inside.

While Long Branch was an exclusive summer playground for the favored few, it gained national fame for a very different reason during the first week of September in 1881.

On July 2, 1881, James A. Garfield, the twentieth president of the United States, was preparing to leave Washington for commencement ceremonies at Williams College, his alma mater. With Garfield was his secretary of state, James G. Blaine. His secretary of war, Robert Todd Lincoln, the oldest son of Abraham Lincoln, was supposed to make the trip as well, but arrived at the station only to explain to Garfield that he could not do so.

As Garfield and Blaine strolled through the Baltimore & Potomac station, they were approached from behind by Charles Guiteau, a disgruntled citizen who had tried and failed to win an election for a local office. Guiteau was armed with a .44 caliber pistol. He took two shots at Garfield. One grazed the president; the other ripped through his right side. Garfield was brought back to the White House where doctors tried to locate the bullet. Although thousands of Civil War veterans were walking around with either bullets or shrapnel as a permanent part of their anatomy, White House doctors were determined to remove the Guiteau slug from the president's side. As they probed to find the bullet, they introduced infection—sterile techniques were just being introduced at about the same time in Europe.

His temperature soared, compounded by a typical brutally hot and humid summer in Washington. His doctors wanted to get him to a cooler climate and, since Garfield had spent a number of summers in Long Branch, it was the logical choice. There was one problem, however. Garfield was weak, but well enough to travel by train. But his doctors feared that a bumpy carriage ride—no matter how short a distance—might do him in. Transporting Garfield from Washington to the Elberon station was no problem. It was the final three-quarters of a mile from the station to the cottage of Charles G. Francklyn, a friend of Garfield's and a shipping baron, that worried the doctors. The solution was simple and not so simple. Build a railway spur from the Elberon station to the Francklyn cottage. The sooner the better.

A force of about two thousand volunteers and railroad workers was organized and work began on the spur on September 4th. Twenty-four hours later, it was done. Garfield arrived in Long Branch that day. The nation, which had been following the Garfield saga, applauded and held out hope for a sea breeze—aided recovery for the president. It didn't happen. Garfield's condition continued to deteriorate, and on September 19, 1881, he passed away.

More macabre trivia: Lincoln, who was not present at Ford's Theater the night his father was shot by John Wilkes Booth, witnessed the Garfield shooting. Twenty-one years later, Lincoln was at the Pan American Exposition in Buffalo to meet President William McKinley, and arrived seconds after

McKinley was mortally wounded by anarchist Leon Czolgoz.

The controversy surrounding his medical care continued. While the nation mourned, Garfield's doctors came under fire. The criticism became so widespread that news of it even reached Guiteau in his jail cell.

At his trial, when asked if he was guilty of murdering the president, Guiteau blamed the doctors. "They did that," he said. "I simply shot him."

Of course that didn't wash with the jury. Guiteau was convicted and executed for the crime.

Garfield is remembered with a monument on Garfield Road, which runs parallel to Ocean Avenue and the oceanfront. The marker, which is on the spot of the old Francklyn Cottage where Garfield died, is on private property, but it is right next to the road. The owner of the new home there doesn't mind people stopping by to look at the monument, but asked that the address not be published. "Ever since I moved right on the beach, I have enough new friends," he said.

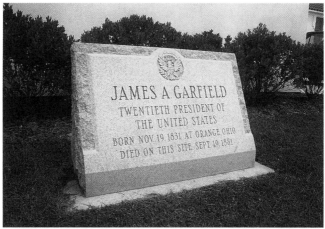

The James Garfield monument in Elberon. Courtesy of The Star-Ledger.

United State Army Communications-Electronics Museum

Kaplan Hall, Building 275
Off Avenue of Memories
Fort Monmouth

OPEN: Monday to Friday: NOON to 4 P.M.

COST: Free.

DIRECTIONS: Take the Garden State Parkway to Exit 105.
Take Route 36 east to Route 35 north, which leads to
the entrance to the Fort.

🐟 Fort Monmouth started up during World War I as an Army Signal Corps development center. Communications technology has changed a great deal since then, and many of the changes began at the fort. According to author John Cunningham in *This is New Jersey* (Rutgers University Press), there are at least forty electronics and communications firms in the Fort Monmouth area that have either manufactured or serviced equipment that was developed at the Fort, or facilitated the communications-electronics industry as a whole.

There have been many communications firsts connected with Monmouth: Major Edwin Armstrong was the first to discover AM and FM radio frequencies; the first radar waves to bounce off the moon came from Camp Evans, a Fort Monmouth outpost in Wall Township, on January 10, 1946.

The Fort Monmouth Communications-Electronic Museum traces many of these developments. There is an exhibit of early vacuum tubes, early radar sets, a case of Armstrong's equipment, battlefield sensors, captured enemy electronics equipment, and, in front of the museum, a display of large mobile telecom equipment, including satellite dishes and a tank.

The museum also has a wing dedicated to the homing pigeon, those early airborne messengers who crossed enemy lines at the drop of a . . . never mind.

One such bird is immortalized there: Hero pigeon G.I. Joe,

stuffed and glass-eyed, is credited with saving as many as a thousand British soldiers who were being shelled with friendly fire during fighting in Italy during World War II.

G.I. Joe, banded with a message that probably said something like "Hold Your Fire!" flew twenty miles in twenty minutes and spared the ground troops further air support.

The museum is closer to the Oceanport Avenue entrance, but from the main entrance of the Fort at Route 35 and Tinton Avenue, follow Avenue of Memories (the main road) past the ballfields and World War II monument. Look for the tank and big telecom equipment. The museum is in an old theater, right next to the base fire house.

Ocean Grove

> DIRECTIONS: Take the Garden State Parkway to Exit 100B. Follow Route 33 east to the junction of state highway 71. Ocean Grove's main entrance is at the junction of the two roads.

✦ When Methodist minister Dr. William B. Osborn, the founder of Ocean Grove, was looking for a place to hold a summertime spiritual and physical revival, he wanted two things: seclusion and a mosquito-free environment. He found it in a square-mile block of seaside land, bordered by two fresh water lakes. The groves of cedar, hickory, and pine trees on the land made choosing a name easy.

In the summer of 1869, a small group of families came for camp. On December 22, 1869, Dr. Osborn and twenty-five other ministers and church members formed the Ocean Grove Camp Meeting Association. The written goal was this: "for the purpose of providing and maintaining, for the members and friends of the Methodist Episcopal Church, a proper, convenient, and desirable permanent Camp Meeting ground and Christian seaside resort."

No matter how optimistic the charter members were about their new venture, they couldn't have possibly imagined how successful, or enduring, it would be.

That first camp meeting attracted about thirty families, who pitched tents in the grove. By the end of 1871, sixty cottages were built with many more families staying, true to the word *camp,* in tents. Demand grew. The lots that sold for fifty dollars in 1870, where selling for thirty times that amount by 1875. By 1880 the Camp Meeting Association constructed a three thousand-seat auditorium to accommodate worshipers. A decade later, Ocean Grove leaders knew a bigger venue was needed and plans were drawn for the Great Auditorium, which originally seated ten thousand. The giant structure was completed by 1894 at a cost of $69,112, and the Camp Meeting Association centered its twentieth anniversary celebrations around the auditorium's opening.

The quick growth of Ocean Grove as a summer spiritual

The first Methodist "Camp Meeting" at Ocean Grove was held in tents. The tradition continues today. Courtesy of The Star-Ledger.

retreat gave rise to a number of other like-communities. Belmar was founded by Ocean Grove summer residents who were looking for a less crowded place. Avon-by-the-Sea was developed as the "Baptist Ocean Grove." Atlantic Highlands was a desired camp meeting location for Methodist ministers. Methodist minister S. Wesley Lake visited Ocean Grove in 1879 and founded Ocean City as a respite from the "bar-rooms, lager beer saloons, cigar shops" of Atlantic City.

Only Ocean Grove has survived with its intent intact. It is the last of the camp-meeting towns on the Jersey Shore. It also made the National Register of Historic Places for its Historic District which, according to a tourism brochure, boasts "the largest aggregate of Victoriana in the country." And yes, that includes Cape May.

Everything in Ocean Grove is within walking distance of the main business district—Main Avenue. It's a great place for a spring or fall day at the beach, before the crowds arrive.

The parklike Ocean Pathway is an impressive row of brightly painted Victorian cottages. Pilgrim Pathway is an open-air market of Ocean Grove history. The Great Auditorium, the Tent Colony, the Bishop Janes Tabernacle, the Thornley Chapel, and even the little Victorian tower that houses the town's tourism office are along this center aisle of Ocean Grove's past. There are hidden architectural treasures everywhere: from the carousel house at the north end of boardwalk to the many Victorian inns throughout the town.

Information about events in Ocean Grove can be obtained by writing to either the Camp Meeting Association or the Ocean Grove Tourism Information Bureau.

> The Camp Meeting Association
> 54 Pitman Avenue, Box 126
> Ocean Grove, NJ 07756.
> PHONE: (908) 775-0035.

The Tourism Information Bureau
P.O. Box 227
Ocean Grove, NJ 07756
PHONE: (908) 774-4736

Staffers at both places are helpful and sincerely interested in both the history and promotion of the town, and there is no shortage of brochures, pamphlets, and other written material.

In the meantime, here is a quick run-through Ocean Grove:

The Great Auditorium

Pilgrim Pathway

The doors to the Great Auditorium are often open. Maintenance work on the football field–sized wooden structure is never ending. There are no organized tours of the building, and its heavy summer schedule of religious and entertainment events often restricts entry to the building to ticket-holders only.

The auditorium, which originally seated ten thousand on bleacher seats, now seats sixty-five hundred in more comfortable theater-type seats. Even with it's reduced capacity, it quietly remains one of the state's largest entertainment venues. By contrast, the new, much ballyhooed New Jersey Performing Arts Center in Newark seats twenty-seven hundred.

Certainly, its honor roll of speakers and performers is second to none. The building has hosted seven presidents—Ulysses S. Grant, James A. Garfield, Williams McKinley, Theodore Roosevelt, William Taft, Woodrow Wilson, and Richard Nixon—and nearly every New Jersey governor. Billy Graham and Norman Vincent Peale have spoken there. So have Lowell Thomas and William Jennings Bryan and Booker T. Washington. Enrico Caruso gave his first American concert there, and John Philip Sousa came to raise the rafters with his band.

In seasons past, the auditorium has hosted entertainment acts from Ricky Scaggs to Neil Sedaka to Tony Bennett, from the Kingston Trio to the Preservation Hall Jazz Band to the New Jersey Symphony Orchestra. Guest evangelists have included Tony Campolo, William K. Quick, and Ronald Irwin of the Salvation Army.

The Great Auditorium is also home to the first organ built by Robert Hope-Jones in America. Hope-Jones, acknowledged as a master (bordering on genius) of his craft also built the organs of England's Worcester Cathedral and St. George's Church in London. The Great Auditorium organ, with 4,200 hundred pipes in 125 ranks is custom-made for the building and designed to complement the building's acoustics. The organ is regarded by experts as one of the most powerful in the United States. Free organ recitals are given in the summer by resident organist Dr. Gordon Turk every Wednesday at 7:30 P.M. and each Saturday at 4 P.M.

Here are some other Great Auditorium facts:

While the great organ can quake the wooden beams in the Great Auditorium, the acoustics are such that a normal conversation at the altar can be overheard clearly by an eavesdropper on the other side of the building.

Another remarkable engineering feat of the antique building is its cooling system. There is none—no heat, either—but even a full capacity audience on a hot, humid August night can be comfortable because of the air exchange inside. Ocean breezes bring fresh air into the 98 doors on the ground-floor level of the building, and the hot stagnant air inside is forced up and out of the balcony windows, of which there are 262 throughout the building.

The words "Be Ye Holy unto the Lord" are painted in a not-so-subtle size under the balcony, lest anyone forget why they came to the Great Auditorium in the first place.

The giant electric American flag above the organ is controlled by the organist. The hundreds of little light bulbs in the flag flicker sequentially, giving the flag a rippling effect when turned on.

The ceiling is fifty-five feet high in the center, and there are six hundred lights in it. The roof is stainless steel, replacing the original corrugated metal roof at a cost of $850,000 in 1988.

The decorative altar rail is 114-feet long and was, at one time, covered by plywood in an attempt to make the building more modern in the 1960s.

The largest of the three towers in front tops off at 131-feet. At the center is a 25-foot cross, which is lit up at night. The cross serves as a beacon for those at sea, who have an unobstructed view of it.

The Tent Colony

In the blocks surrounding the Great Auditorium are the 114 tents the Camp Meeting Association rents out each summer, a throwback to the first days of Ocean Grove. The tents are stored in permanent wood sheds on each lot, then pulled out and pitched for the season. The uniform peaks, flowers boxes, and colorful awnings give the tent neighborhood the same look as the Victorian row along Ocean Pathway, just in a more simple miniature. Residents plant garden in front, where they often sit in lawn chairs. It is as friendly a neighborhood as you'll find and, despite the close quarters, quiet and peaceful.

The Bishop Janes Tabernacle
Pilgrim Pathway

The tabernacle dates back to 1877, making it the oldest house of worship in Ocean Grove. Janes Tabernacle is home to most of the daily 9 A.M. Bible hours during the summer. Ocean Grove is one the few places left where most people still dress formally for church, even on a weekday in August. After services, the churchgoers congregate in the park outside of Janes Tabernacle, to talk over more earthly matters. The tabernacle, a respectable size for any community church, is dwarfed by the Great Auditorium right next door, but like it's bigger, younger cousin, it is a very simple, very elegant, and very beautiful building.

The tabernacle is closed to the public when services are not in session.

The Thornley Chapel

Pilgrim Pathway

 The chapel, built in 1889, is named for Joseph H. Thornley, a charter member of the Camp Meeting Association. It was Thornley who hosted the first religious service in Ocean Grove, when he opened his tent to fellow worshipers on July 31, 1889. The chapel opened in the summer of 1889, three months after Thornley's death. The little chapel is the center of children's activities in the summer. Off-season, the Camp Meeting Association opens it as a drop-in center for the developmentally disabled and mentally ill people who live in the town.

Ocean Grove, with its many high occupancy boarding homes, has been a favored spot to send people who are being deinstitutionalized. For one, the town is safe, with virtually no street criminals to prey on the disadvantaged. Second, the density of housing and its proximity to town and services makes it convenient for people unable to travel in too wide a circle. The placement of these people in Ocean Grove is a hot topic in town. Many people feel that the boarding house operators who take state subsidies to house the people, don't do enough to care for them once they're there, and that the sight of disheveled people wandering aimlessly around town is bad for the town image. The prevailing sentiment is that the state should keep the people in institutions, where they will get better care. It's a tough issue. The people of Ocean Grove want to show compassion—there but for the grace of God go I—but are afraid of the effect these people have on tourism and, ultimately, the future of the town. One woman who works promoting the town said she overheard a couple talking about "going back to Cape May" after seeing a few mentally ill people on the street. "We can't let that happen," she said. "This town is too beautiful to have that happen."

Centennial Cottage

Corner of Central Avenue and McClintock Streets
Ocean Grove
(908) 775-1969

OPEN: July and August, Monday through Saturday: 11 A.M. to 3 P.M.; June and September, Saturdays: 11 A.M. to 3 P.M. The unheated cottage has no off-season hours.

COST: Adults, $1.00. Children, 25 cents.

The Centennial Cottage was built in 1874 by the Fels family of Fels-Naptha Soap fame on the south side of town and moved to its current location for Ocean Grove's centennial celebration in 1969.

The two-story cottage was restored and furnished to depict the domestic life of well-to-do families in the early days of Ocean Grove. Every piece of furniture dates back to the late 1800s. The exterior woodwork replicates the Victorian Gothic style of the day. The people of the 1870s may have lacked certain creature comforts, but they knew how to surround themselves with well-crafted things of beauty.

Centennial Cottage is an authentic period piece through and through—hence, no heat—right down to the Victorian garden out back filled with flowers, herbs, shrubs, and trees that were popular in post–Civil War America.

The Ocean Grove Historical Museum

Ocean Grove Camp Meeting Association
54 Pitman Avenue
Ocean Grove
(908) 774-1869

OPEN: Summers: Tuesdays and Wednesdays: 1 P.M. to 4 P.M., and Saturdays: 9 A.M. to 3 P.M. The museum is closed from November 1 to May 1; late spring and early fall hours are Wednesdays: 1 P.M. to 4 P.M. and Saturdays: 9 A.M. to 3 P.M. The museum is also open by appointment. Call (908) 774-1869.

COST: Free.

The museum is in the building that houses the Camp Meeting Association, but is only staffed by volunteers at the above times. The museum captures the flavor of old-time Ocean Grove, right down to the iron ice cream molds used at Day's Ice Cream Parlor and the ticket box from the Strand Theater. There is also a large postcard and stereopticon slide collection. Another impressive piece of Ocean Grove memorabilia is Silver Star, one of the horses from the Ocean Grove carousel. The museum also has changing exhibits: a recent one was about the ushers at the Great Auditorium, proof that the historical society has a wealth of photos and other documents and the imagination to use them.

The Spring Lake Historical Society Museum

Spring Lake Municipal Building
Corner of 5th & Warren Avenues
Spring Lake
(908) 449-0772

OPEN: Tuesdays: 10 A.M. to NOON; Sundays: 1 P.M. to 3 P.M. Also by appointment. Call (908) 449-0772

COST: Free. Donations accepted.

DIRECTIONS: Take the Garden State Parkway to Exit 98 and follow to Route 34 south. Take Route 34 south to first circle and follow signs to Spring Lake. This is Allaire Road, which will take you to Route 71. Cross Route 71 into Spring Lake, where road becomes Ludlow Avenue, go over the railroad tracks, and make your first right, which is 5th Avenue. The municipal Building is five blocks ahead.

The Spring Lake Historical Society Museum, like the town itself, is one of the hidden treasures of the shore. It is a professionally installed museum, laid out in a very organized, chronological time-line of town history.

The museum does its job in covering the two histories and two images of Spring Lake.

The first, brought to the public's attention by catch-descriptions like "The Irish Riviera" and "The Short Hills of the Shore," is of a summer playground for the rich and upscale weekenders.

The second image, unbeknownst to most of the people who weekend at the many Victorian bed-and-breakfasts or the few remaining oceanfront hotels, is of a solid small town, with a strong volunteer fire department and first-aid squad—one of the oldest in the state—and a VFW hall. A town filled with year-round residents who do not catch the train each morning for Wall Street, but work in places like local banks, or at Fort Monmouth, or the Navy's Earle Ammunition Depot, or open up their own stores along Third Avenue every morning. This Spring Lake was inhabited by farmers and fishermen in the late 1700s, by railroad workers and masons and handymen in the late 1800s.

These were the people who paved the roads and built the great hotels and seaside "cottages." They fought the great fire of 1900—which wiped out four hotels and most of the area's business district, which in those days was closer to the ocean. They were the people who rebuilt the town after the disaster, and did it again after the fire of 1901, which took down the Sussex Hotel, and again after the fire of 1909, which destroyed the Breakers Hotel.

They were the regular people, the shopkeepers, the icemen, the stablehands, the people who did the work in the seashore developments of Villa Park, Spring Lake Beach, Como, and Brighton–North Brighton, which merged to form Spring Lake.

They were also the people whose actions were no less heroic on the morning of September 8, 1934, when another fire disaster visited Spring Lake's shores. This time, the fire was out at sea, aboard the luxury liner *Morro Castle*, which was returning to New York from a Cuban "whoopie" cruise. As the 508-foot liner listed helplessly off Spring Lake beach, the flames being fanned by the winds of a nor'easter, the relentless wail of emergency whistles were waking up the year-round residents of Spring Lake. Word spread quickly that the *Morro Castle*—familiar to residents through newspaper ads, radio commercials, and frequent sightings off shore as it steamed out of New York Harbor and headed south—was burning. Rescue workers and other good Samaritans rushed to the beach in time to pull in the first two lifeboats, which were carrying mostly crew members. As the flames engulfed the ship, passengers were faced with a grim choice: jump ship and risk drowning in the storm-whipped seas, or stay aboard and risk burning to death. Most passengers opted for the former, and did their best to swim in from the burning ship, a mile-and-a-half out at sea.

On shore, Spring Lake volunteers like Stanley Truax, who, as he nears eighty, is still a member of the town's first-aid squad, waded into the surf to pull in survivors, and later, the bodies of the dead.

"It was an ungodly sight," Truax said. "You could see people jumping, one after another, like monkeys from a tree. They just kept jumping."

Truax remembers pulling in a naked girl, covering her with

his overcoat, and driving her to the makeshift emergency room at police headquarters. He returned to the beach, without the coat, and spent the next six hours in the surf.

"It was exhausting, but those people needed help, so you just kept going," he said.

Many residents worked the beach, others transported injured, and others went door-to-door for medical supplies and blankets.

"Blankets were the big thing," said lifetime resident Jerry Tricarico, who was nine at the time of the disaster. "Those people were freezing when they finally got in."

The museum has a small section devoted to the *Morro Castle,* with a montage of photographs, an oar from a lifeboat, a life preserver, a first-aid squad jumpsuit, and other memorabilia from the ship.

The most striking photographs in the Spring Lake museum collection are not of the *Morro Castle.* They are of the March

The Morro Castle *burned off Spring Lake and was being towed to New York when she broke loose and washed up at Asbury Park. Courtesy of Newark Public Library.*

1975 tear-down of the red-domed Monmouth Hotel. The hotel, built in 1904, had five hundred rooms and took up a full block. The gardens faced the lake, the nearly three hundred-foot frontage, anchored by the colossal pillars of the entrance, faced the ocean. The photographs of the great dome being toppled are disturbing as they dramatically convey the end of an era. Nearby is a photo of the Monmouth, with the German airship Hindenburg hovering over it (see in *Ocean County*). Two monumental architectural and engineering wonders, equally doomed.

The image of Spring Lake as a millionaire's summer paradise is well-documented in the first room of the museum, which is devoted to Martin Maloney, a public utilities bigwig from Philadelphia and papal marquis, who, in many ways, was the patron saint of Spring Lake.

He was certainly responsible for two of the town landmarks: the glorious St. Catharine's Church which stands on a postcard-like setting next to the lake, and his summer estate, Ballingarry, which cost eight million dollars to build and was dubbed the White House by the Sea, because of its resemblance in size and splendor to the president's home in Washington.

St. Catharine's, which resembles St. Peter's Basilica in Rome, was born from Maloney's grief over losing his daughter Catharine, known as Kitty, to tuberculosis at age seventeen. Maloney offered to donate a church in her memory, and the cornerstone for the miniature cathedral was laid in 1901. The church took twenty-five years to build, and artists and craftsmen were imported from Europe to make it an authentic old-world house of worship. The frescoes and canvas murals were painted by Gonippo Raggi, a graduate of St. Luke's Academy of Fine Art in Rome. The stained-glass windows and Stations of the Cross were made by Mayer & Co. of Bavaria. Maloney did not live to see the church completed. He died on

May 8, 1921, and his remains are at St. Catharine's, in the Maloney family mausoleum.

St. Catharine's has recently undergone an extensive renovation, including a new copper roof. Now the church, which is the most enduring symbol of the town's picturesque beauty, is ready for the next century.

Ballingarry was taken down in 1953, one of the last great estates that sprung up in Spring Lake during the latter part of the 1800s. But part of the iron fence that surrounded the estate and much of the brickwork of the extensive gardens still stand on the block formed by First, Second, Jersey, and Morris avenues, a more subtle reminder of Maloney's impact on the town.

Ocean County

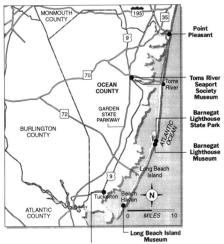

MONMOUTH COUNTY

195

35

9

Point Pleasant

70

OCEAN COUNTY

Toms River

Toms River Seaport Society Museum

GARDEN STATE PARKWAY

72

BURLINGTON COUNTY

Barnegat Lighthouse State Park

ATLANTIC OCEAN

Barnegat Lighthouse Museum

9

Long Beach Island

Tuckerton

Beach Haven

N

ATLANTIC COUNTY

0   MILES   10

Long Beach Island Museum

Barnegat Bay Decoy and Baymen's Museum

Ocean County is New Jersey's own "sportsman's paradise," from fishing and crabbing in the Barnegat Bay and the Atlantic Ocean, to duck hunting in the Tuckerton area. Other "sportsmen"—and women—enjoy the county too. The Pinelands begin here, giving hikers an infinite number of options for exploration. Bird watchers flock to the wetlands. And they say the wind surfing in the Barnegat Bay just off South Seaside is unequaled in the world. Originally part of Monmouth, Ocean County carved out its own identity with work, not play. It was home to one of New Jersey's largest ship-building industries and was the leading producer of bog iron. In the days before refrigeration, salt was the primary way to preserve food, and the salt works in the Toms River area helped keep the nation well fed. The county has a colorful litany of myth and history. Pirates hid there during the Revolution. Babe Ruth hunted there in the 1920s. Storms devoured the coast line, and the Jersey Devil devoured chickens and other small animals throughout the county's pinelands. But the single biggest event to ever hit Ocean County was the explosion and crash of the *Hindenburg* on May 6, 1932, as it came in for a landing at the Lakehurst Naval Air Station. The disaster killed thirty-six people and also put an immediate end to airship travel.

Toms River Seaport Society Museum

Hooper Avenue and East Water Streets
Toms River
(908) 349-9209

OPEN: Tuesdays and Saturdays: 10 A.M. to 2 P.M., and by appointment.

COST: Donations accepted.

DIRECTIONS: Take the Garden State Parkway to Exit 81 and go east on Water Street. Make a left on Hooper Avenue. The museum is on the right.

The Toms River Seaport Society Museum is set up like an old-time boatyard. Crews of volunteers restore boats that have been donated to the museum, and once done, they are set up for display.

"We are taking small boats that are indigenous to the area and restoring them," said museum director Ed Asay. "These are boats you would see used in the Barnegat Bay."

The society owns over twenty crafts, some restored, others in the process of being restored, and others on the waiting list. The boats are set up outside the workshop area of the museum, and each has a small identification card. The boats most commonly associated with the Barnegat Bay area are the Barnegat Bay Sneak Boxes and the Sea Bright Skiffs.

The Sneak Box seems to have been invented by Hazelton Seaman of West Creek, down by Tuckerton, around 1836. The small, maneuverable boat was designed to allow hunters to sneak up on ducks in the shallow marshes of the Barnegat Bay. The hunter would sit on the floor of the boat, essentially blending in with the scenery and guide the craft silently through the dawn. Because the boat can operate in shallow waters, a hunter could actually move into the grassy areas of the marsh or river banks and become camouflaged. Once the Sneak Box were hidden in the grasses, all the hunter needed was a few duck decoys and a little patience. Of course, the whole clandestine operation

Boat restorers at work at the Toms River Seaport Society Museum. Courtesy of The Star-Ledger.

would end as soon as a group of ducks appeared within target range. Then the silent dawn would be shattered by the blast of a shotgun.

It was J. Howard Perrine of Barnegat who turned the Sneak Box into what Asay calls the "the Model T of sailing."

"When J. Howard Perrine of Barnegat began building these little boats, sailing became an affordable pastime for most people. Suddenly everyone could afford a boat."

And suddenly, Sneak Boxes weren't just for hunters. Perrine tapped into the recreational boating market, and his boat works, started around the turn of the century, was built up to respond to the demand. Sneak Boxes, the invention of one craftsman's passion for hunting, were now rolled out assembly-line style. One of Perrine's boat builders was Sam Hunt of Waretown, who is in his eighties today. Hunt continues to build Sneak Boxes out of wood, a craftsman working alone in a one-hundred-fifty-year-old tradition. His story is told in *Down the Jersey Shore* by Russell Roberts and Rich Youmans (Rutgers University Press, 1993).

The Seaport Society owns a 1902 Perrine Sneak Box, but their most famous Sneak Box is the *Sheldrake,* which was sailed from New York to Miami down the intracoastal waterway in 1925.

The Sea Bright Skiff also dates back to the 1800s, when Jersey Shore fishermen needed a rugged, stable boat to cut through the surf. The boat's sharp stern helped it break through the waves, but its flat bottom allowed it to be launched from the beach. When fishermen would return with their sea bounty, the boat could wash up on shore without tipping over.

The resort boom of the mid- to late 1800s at the shore gave the skiff a new purpose, as a lifeguard's boat. The skiff is used today on virtually every beach that has a lifeguard staff, although most new skiffs are made out of lighter, more durable fiberglass.

The Hankins family was New Jersey's most notable skiff builders. Charles Hankins of Lavalette (see New Jersey Folklife Center, *Cumberland County*) may be one of New Jersey's most famous craftsmen. Countless articles have been written about him, and a PBS documentary followed. Robert and Youmans also write extensively about Hankins in *Down the Jersey Shore.*

Hankins is semiretired now, working alone in a shop that is a virtual tool museum. Hankins builds boats the way his father taught him to do in the 1930s, using only cedar and oak and tools that are no longer manufactured. Since 1946, when Hankins returned from World War II and took over the family business, he estimates he and his helpers have built four thousand boats—an average of eighty a year.

Hankins wasn't the only skiff builder. There were dozens of shops along the coast and the Seaport Society Museum has a number of examples of these skiffs.

Inside the museum, there is a maritime library with over six thousand volumes and over one thousand artifacts, including a display of half-models and the coast's best display of intricate marlinespike, the art of knot and line tying.

There are also a sextant collection, antique sailing trophies, a collection of caulking irons and other boat-building tools, and a number of highly decorative sea chests.

The museum itself is in a historically significant building. It is in the former carriage house on the Joseph Francis estate—the main house is gone, replaced by a riverfront condominium complex. While Dr. William A. Newell of Manahawkin is credited with creating the U.S. Lifesaving Service, Joseph Francis invented the most valuable tool in the fight to save lives against raging seas. Newell designed the ship to shore line, which would be fired from a small cannon from the beach onto a stricken ship off shore. The breeches buoy, a sturdy canvas seat resembling short pants shown into a life preserver, would be run out between ship and shore, bringing in one crewman or passenger at a time. Lifeboats were also used, but extremely dangerous in times of the high, turbulent seas that were the cause of the many groundings and wrecks in the first place.

Francis, a lifelong maritime inventor who developed the unsinkable row boat—with corks in bow and stern—came up with a better idea: a small, airtight metal "boat" that could be reeled out on the line and pulled back in. It was called the Lifecar (see Twin Lights, *Monmouth County*). The metal car could withstand the sea's pounding, and the airtight hatch would keep it from sinking. It was almost perfect. The only drawback was that the Lifecar could only hold two average-sized people comfortably, although four or five, including children, could be crammed in.

The Lifecar was an instant success. When the British passenger ship *Ayrshire* got stuck on a shoal three hundred yards off Barnegat Island during a blizzard in January of 1850, the Lifecar safely brought in two hundred of the two hundred and one passengers over the next two days. The lone casualty was a man who tried to cling to the outside of the car while his family was inside. He was washed away.

For a good example of the continuing maritime traditions in Ocean County, visit the Manasquan Inlet area of Point Pleasant. Here you'll find a commercial fishing fleet and fishermen's cooperative, as well as charter fishing boats and every imaginable size of pleasure craft. Take the Garden State Parkway to Route 34 South, follow about seven miles to the bridge that goes over the Manasquan Inlet. Turn left at the end of the bridge into Point Pleasant.

Barnegat Lighthouse State Park

Northern tip of Long Beach Island
Barnegat Light
(609) 494-2016

OPEN: THE PARK is open daily at 8 A.M., but closing times vary throughout the year. From May 1 to Memorial Day, the park closes at 8 P.M. From Memorial Day through Labor Day, the park closes at 10 P.M. From Labor Day until the end of September, the park closes at 8 P.M. During October, the park closes at 6 P.M. During the winter, the park closes at 4 P.M.

THE LIGHTHOUSE is open from May 1 to Memorial Day on weekends only, from 9 A.M. to 4:30 P.M. From Memorial Day until Labor Day the lighthouse is open every day from 9 A.M. to 4:30 P.M. From Labor Day through the end of October the lighthouse is open on weekends only, from 9 A.M. to 4:30 P.M. The lighthouse is closed from the end of October to the beginning of May. They are considering extending spring and fall hours in the near future.

COST: Park is free. Lighthouse is $1 for adults, and children under 12 are free.

DIRECTIONS: Take the Garden State Parkway to Exit 63, then follow Route 72 east over the bridge onto Long Beach Island. Go north on Boulevard for about 8 miles. Follow the signs to lighthouse.

The architect would go on to become a Civil War hero. His lighthouse would go on to help end the ship carnage off of Long Beach Island's treacherous coast. The lighthouse itself would become vulnerable to the sea, in danger of being wrecked and washed away, like it's doomed predecessor. When the government no longer cared, the citizens and sailors who nicknamed it Old Barney would come to its rescue.

With a history like that, it's surprising the Barnegat Lighthouse hasn't been made into a TV movie. It has, however, been made into thousands of postcards. Its picture has been used on book covers, calendars, coffee mugs, T-shirts, and anything else that needs authentic seashore adornment.

Research Old Barney and one common theme keeps popping up: many authors have called it the New Jersey Shore's most famous landmark. Towering 180-feet above sea level, it is certainly one of the most prominent . . . a kind of Empire State Building of the coastal skyline. Shore visitors can get a good view of Old Barney from most parts of northernmost Long Beach Island, or from Island Beach State Park, which is across the Barnegat Inlet.

The lighthouse's presence certainly made an impact on men at sea. The Ocean County barrier islands—Long Beach Island and Barnegat Beach Island, the island to the north which stretches from Point Pleasant to Island Beach State Park—were especially troublesome for navigators. About two hundred and fifty ships were lost off the barrier islands between 1800 and 1840. Dr. William A. Newell witnessed one of the wrecks during a hurricane on August 13, 1839, and was so moved by not only the loss of life, but the helplessness he felt standing on shore, that he began relentlessly petitioning for an organized life-saving service. He was elected to Congress and twelve years later the U.S. Life Saving Service was created by federal legislation. The Barnegat Lighthouse not only marked the entrance to the Barnegat Inlet, but warned ships to keep their distance from the shoal-laden barrier islands.

Old Barney is actually Young Barney. The first lighthouse at the inlet was built in 1834. It was only about forty feet tall, dramatically lowering its at-sea visibility. Worse yet, it did not have a flashing light, and captains at sea could not be sure if the light they were seeing was the lighthouse or a ship closer to the coast. The lighthouse was inadequate, but before critics could succeed in getting it replaced, the sea did their demolition work for them. By 1856 it was gone, brought down by the same sea that had claimed so many ships along the stretch.

Lt. George Meade, an engineering officer with the U.S. Army, was given the job of building a new lighthouse. Meade came up with two plans—a state-of-the-art lighthouse and an economy model. He then went on to successfully lobby Congress for the better building. Meade's tower is 27-feet wide at its base, gradually tapering to 15-feet wide at its top. It is double walled, designed to allow air to flow between both walls, cutting down on potential moisture rot of the bricks. The tower is also designed to sway with the wind—the bend-don't-break philosophy later used by skyscraper architects. There are 217 steps in the spiral staircase that goes from the base to the lantern room. Meade, who would later command Union forces at the Battle of Gettysburg, ordered a top-of-the-line lens with 24 flash panels, making it the strongest signal on the Jersey Coast.

The new Barnegat Lighthouse went on line in January of 1859. Although it was built nine hundred feet from the ocean, by 1866 the sea had cut the distance in half. A Victorian cottage was built in 1889 for the lightkeepers and their families but was

Parts of the Barnegat Bay are still desolate in winter. Courtesy of Newark Public Library.

consumed by the sea in 1920. By 1927 the tower itself was threatened, and the lighthouse was de-emphasized in favor of an offshore lightship. The valuable original lens was dismantled and moved, and a lesser light replaced it. The people of Long Beach Island, sensing the government was giving up on Old Barney, decided to fight the erosion on their own and made a makeshift jetty of junked automobiles. It wasn't until the 1940s that the government showed any interest in saving the landmark. The U.S. Army Corps of Engineers came in and built two jetties and a dike to slow the erosion.

The government then moved into Old Barney, using it as a lookout for German submarines during World War II. The state took Old Barney over in 1956 and created a park around it, saving it from neglect and eventual decay.

The state takes Old Barney's health seriously. The erosion near the lighthouse is under constant surveillance and, in 1988, the state began a massive two-year restoration project. The lighthouse was closed until 1991 while structural repairs were underway, and just before it re-opened, it was given a new coat of paint—red on top and white below, just as Lt. Meade had ordered a hundred and twenty years before.

Barnegat Light Museum

> 5th St. and Central Ave.
> Barnegat Light
> (609) 494-8578

OPEN: In July and August, daily: 2 P.M. to 5 P.M. In June and September, Saturdays and Sundays: 2 P.M. to 5 P.M.

COST: Donations accepted.

DIRECTIONS: Take the Garden State Parkway to Exit 63, then follow Route 72 east over the bridge onto Long Beach Island. Go north on Boulevard for about 8 miles and make a left on 5th St. The museum is one block up on left.

Sinbad is buried at the old 6th Street Coast Guard Station, a small headstone underneath the flag pole marks his final resting place. He was Barnegat Light's most famous animal, and an exhibit at the town museum tell why.

It seems Sinbad, a part-Rotweiler mutt, was smuggled aboard the Coast Guard cutter *Campbell* during World War II. The dog became the crew's mascot, standing by them as they endured storms and shellings, and anything else nature and the Axis powers could muster up. The ship, crew, and dog came through the war basically unscathed, and the superstitious sailors said it was all because of Sinbad.

Sinbad was decorated with all the service ribbons regular crew members received, which he wore proudly on his collar. Stories of his exploits were written up in *Life* magazine and *Reader's Digest.* Sinbad lived out his life at the Barnegat Light Coast Guard Station, and today has his own section of the museum. His legacy also lives on aboard the Coast Guard cutter *Campbell II,* which has a bronze statue of Sinbad in the mess hall . . . just in case he really was a good luck charm.

As interesting as the Sinbad story is, the main attraction at the museum is the original lens from the Barnegat Lighthouse. The giant lens is a series of over a thousand prisms mounted on brass frames, made in 1847 by the St. Gabian works near Paris. The lens threw off a beam that could be seen 30 miles at sea on a clear night, and only the curvature of the earth made it impossible to see from further out.

The lens and clockwork mechanism that rotated it weighed over five tons. In severe storms, when the sway of the lighthouse threw off the balance of the rotating mechanism, the lightkeeper could move the entire lens by hand, thanks to a set of bronze rollers.

The museum, a former one-room schoolhouse built in 1903, has many photographs of Old Barney through the years, including pictures of the wick house and lightkeeper's cottage, which was washed out to sea in 1920.

The museum also has pieces of ships that were wrecked along the coast and other nautical artifacts, such as ships' compasses and sextants. There is an antique replica of a pound net, used by island fisherman to catch fish from the beach. When the nets were full, a team of horses would pull them in.

The museum also remembers the two big hotels in the area, the Oceanic and Sunset, with pictures and items of furniture, dishes, silverware, and the like. The two hotels are gone now, having met the fate of so many other large hotels at the shore. The Sunset burned and the Oceanic was washed away.

Long Beach Island Museum

> Engelside and Beach Avenues
> Beach Haven
> (609) 492-0700

OPEN: Summers, daily: 2 P.M. to 4 P.M., then 7 P.M. to 9 P.M. On Tuesdays and Fridays: 10 A.M. to noon, 2 P.M. to 4 P.M., and 7 P.M. to 9 P.M. The museum's summer hours start about the week before Memorial Day and continue until a week past Labor Day. The museum has spring and fall weekend hours of from 2 P.M. to 4 P.M. from about mid-May and closing at the end of September.

COST: $1.50 for adults, 25-cents for children under 12 (except infants, who are free.

DIRECTIONS: Take the Garden State Parkway to Exit 63, then follow Route 72 east over bridge on to Long Beach Island. Go south on Boulevard for 7½ miles and make a left on Engelside. The museum is on the left, across from the park.

There are a wide, block-long park, a stage theater, an ice cream parlor with singing waiters, and a church-turned-museum. Up the street is an old hotel facing the ocean, and the block is lined with giant cedar-shingled guest homes.

The historic district of Beach Haven may be the most picturesque little town on the Jersey Shore. Like Spring Lake (see in *Monmouth County*), the town has retained its small town character and not allowed runaway development to plow under its past or overcrowd its landscape.

There is an amusement area at Beach Haven, but it is inland on the Boulevard. Those with small children will find the one-block Fantasy Island Amusement Park to be the cleanest, most reasonably priced place of its kind along the shore.

Beach Haven was founded as a Quaker summer meeting place in 1870. At the time Quakers came to Long Beach Island, the island was home to only fisherman and a few other hearty souls who didn't mind the isolation or the rough winter environment. The island could only be reached by boat, usually ferried between Tuckerton on the mainland and Tucker's Island, where Reuben Tucker attracted paying guests with a hunting and fishing hotel as early as 1765. If Tucker's Island were not underwater today, it could lay claim to being the nation's

Pound fishermen battle the surf off Long Beach Island in the 1920s. Courtesy of Newark Public Library.

first seaside resort. Instead, Cape May can legitimately claim the title.

By 1870 interest in the barrier islands for resorts was building. Point Pleasant was developing. Baptists settled Seaside as a summer retreat, and Bay Head began to attract wealthy summer clientele.

By the mid-1880s a rail line connected Long Beach Island to the mainland. By 1899 Beach Haven became so built up and crowded in summer, that the newly founded city had to pass ordinances to limit fresh water consumption.

The first summer "cottages" were built in Beach Haven in 1874, one by Archelaus R. Pharo of Tuckerton. His daughter is credited with naming the town Beach Haven. Construction of other summer homes and guest homes quickly followed. By the end of the summer, the Parry House and Beach Haven House were completed, as well as Quakers' Beach Haven Friends Meeting House. By the following year, the first Engelside Hotel, with rooms for three hundred guests, was standing at the ocean's side.

In 1882 the Holy Innocents Episcopal Church, the first in town, was built with money donated by Mrs. Charles Parry.

The fishery houses at Long Beach Island in 1924. Courtesy of Newark Public Library.

Coast Guard patrols the surf at dawn at Beach Haven in the 1920s. Courtesy of Newark Public Library.

Legend has it that she wanted to express her gratitude to God for allowing her to escape the fire which destroyed the Parry House a year earlier.

The years 1890 through 1893 saw Beach Haven grow at a head-spinning pace. A downtown area sprang up, with no less than a dozen stores, including two meat markets, two ice cream parlors, three general stores and a bakery. A mayor was elected; the town was incorporated. A post office was built. A Methodist Church was built. It was still only 1890. Residential building doubled, then tripled, the town's summer population. Beach Haven was on its way to becoming one of the Shore's most popular resorts.

The museum is located in the original Holy Innocents Church (a new one was built in 1974). The museum collection is extensive and covers all of Long Beach Island. You can see the first switchboard that was used on the island or parts of the skeleton of a whale that washed up. The museum acknowledges the island's hunting and fishing past. There's a display of guns, duck decoys, a Sneak Box, and antique rods and tackles and nets.

The most interesting display is the Tucker's Island section. Tucker's Island, originally known as Short Beach, spent the last few centuries being either connected to or disconnected from Long Beach Island, depending on what the sea chose to do. At times the sea rose and created the Beach Haven Inlet (between Beach Haven and Tucker's). Other times, one could walk across the sand and get to the sometimes-island. The island was a modest little resort, catering primarily to sportsmen. In 1848 a two-story Cape Cod lighthouse was built on the island. By 1869 a U.S. Life Saving Service Station was there. The lightkeeper and lifesavers formed the nucleus of a year-round population, and a one-room schoolhouse/community center was built in 1895.

Over the next twenty-five years, however, residents realized their little island was being eaten away. They did the prudent

The wreck of the Fortuna *at Ship Bottom. Long Beach Island was the shipwreck capital of the world in the 1800s. Courtesy of Newark Public Library.*

thing: they got out of there. By the early 1920s, the island was abandoned, a ghost town of buildings waiting to be swept away by the ocean. The lighthouse went down in 1927. The Life Saving Station fell in 1935.

The island is remembered by the museum, a shrine to a long lost brother. There are pictures of life on Tucker's Island in the good old days, and an aerial map of the island as it suffered from consumption. Finally, there are dramatic pictures of the buildings going down, the island's last days as a place, rather than a mere sand shoal jutting off the south end of Long Beach Island.

Barnegat Bay Decoy and Baymen's Museum

137 West Main St. (Route 9)
Tuckerton
(609) 296-8868

OPEN: Wednesdays through Sundays: 10 A.M. to 4:30 P.M.

COST: $2 for adults. Children under 12 are free.

DIRECTIONS: Take the Garden State Parkway to Exit 58. Follow Route 539 south for 4 miles until it intersects with Route 9. Take Route 9 south for ¼ mile. The museum is at the entrance to Tip Seaman County Park.

If you had to pick one place along the New Jersey coast to get a feel for the entire state's maritime history and industries, the Baymen's museum would be your best bet. This is a top-notch, well-financed, professional museum and the first step in the ambitious Tuckerton Seaport Project, which will recapture the spirit of Tuckerton as an important Colonial port.

The museum recalls the days when men worked with their hands, and a family could survive on what the earth gave them. If nothing else, the Baymen's Museum is a shrine to survival. And ingenuity. The collections here prove that man can always adapt to his environment. Over the centuries, settlers in the bay area perfected techniques to catch food from the waters and make salt from the earth's deposits. They developed ships that could overtake British freighters and boats that could sneak up on ducks. Over two centuries, Tuckerton men and women have proved one thing: the hands of the craftsman are the tools of an inventive mind.

There is a Sneak Box built by Josephson Seaman, a descendant of Sneak Box inventor Hazelton Seaman, complete with rigged sail. There are the traditional tools of boat building, net mending, grass shrimping, oystering, eeling, clamming, salt hay harvesting. If it was done for a living in the Tuckerton area, the museum has the tools it was done with.

The museum has a collection of over four thousand photographs, arranged neatly in binders, that record every aspect of Tuckerton daily life, sites, products, and progress since the invention of the camera. You can spend a day looking at these scenes from Tuckerton, old and new.

There is also a sportsmen's section: guns, fishing tackle, nets,

Site of the proposed Tuckerton Seaport. Courtesy of The Star-Ledger.

Barnegat clammers hit rough times in recent decades. Here's a business for sale in 1969. Courtesy of Newark Public Library.

pictures of famous hunting-and-fishing clubs—like the Bayside Inn—with men standing proudly with their guns and racks of taken ducks, or fishermen with lines of caught fish. The area has a rich sportsmen's tradition: in fact, the museum is built as a replica of a classic bay area hunting "shack."

The area's reputation as a prime hunting and fishing ground led to the development of duck decoy carving as a livelihood for native woodworkers—there's that ingenuity again. Tuckerton continues to promote this home-grown traditional craft with an annual duck-decoy show and wildlife art exhibit each September. And if you think the show draws an eclectic handful of folk art enthusiasts, think again. The three-day show draws about fifty thousand people, and attendance is climbing.

The patron saint of carvers and collectors alike is Harry V. Shourds. Harry V. Shourds greets every visitor to the museum. No matter that Harry died in 1920. His spirit lives on at the museum, embodied in a wax figure of Harry that sits in the replica of his decoy-carving shop. Nobody could carve a duck decoy like Harry Shourds. Not then, not now. Shourds carved

Duck carver John Holloway at the Baymen's Museum. Courtesy of
The Star-Ledger.

over fifty thousand decoys in his lifetime, selling them to local duck hunters and tourists who came "gunning" in the bay area.

Like Van Gogh, Shourds had no idea his art would some-day be worth a fortune. Some of Shourds's decoys—depend-ing on the condition and rarity of the bird—are drawing six-figure bids in auctions. The museum has a large number of Shourds's originals in its collection of about a hundred and fifty duck decoys and other carved shorebirds.

While Tuckerton was developing as a sportsmen's paradise, it is was also developing as one of the most important boat building and shipping points on the coast. George Washing-ton officially named it the nation's third port of entry during the Revolution, and American privateers put out from the area to commandeer British cargo ships (see Chestnut Neck Monu-ment, *Atlantic County*).

Within the next few years, Tuckerton's waterfront will have replicated buildings and shops from it's Colonial heyday and the 1800s. Plans to raise ten million dollars for the project are

MARK DI IONNO

The Point Pleasant wharf area, home to a large commercial fishing fleet.

A drawing of the planned reconstruction of the Tucker's Island Lighthouse that will be the centerpiece of the new Tuckerton Seaport.

well on their way, and the 16-acre site is already on the drawing board.

The centerpiece will be a replica of the Tucker's Island Lighthouse, which will house a museum and interpretive center. There will be a dockmaster's shop, a gun club, a pound fishery, an ice house, a railway station and dock, a clam house and oyster house, a replica of the Island Beach Life Saving Service Station (there is also a Life Saving exhibit at the museum), two boat works, and three—yes, three,—duck decoy carving shops. Harry V. Shourds would be proud.

Atlantic County

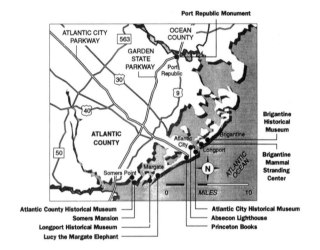

Port Republic Monument

ATLANTIC CITY PARKWAY
563
OCEAN COUNTY
GARDEN STATE PARKWAY
30
Port Republic
9
ATLANTIC COUNTY
40
50
Somers Point
Margate
Atlantic City
Brigantine
Longport
Brigantine Historical Museum
Brigantine Mammal Stranding Center
ATLANTIC OCEAN
N
0 MILES 10

Atlantic County Historical Museum
Somers Mansion
Longport Historical Museum
Lucy the Margate Elephant

Atlantic City Historical Museum
Absecon Lighthouse
Princeton Books

One of the most striking views of the Atlantic City skyline is from the Edwin B. Forsythe Wildlife Management Area across the grassy wetlands and inlets of Absecon Bay. The neon buzz of the East Coast gaming capital is muted by the expanse of water and marshlands. At Forsythe, the only sound you hear is the wind rustling the marsh grasses, and the occasional cry of waterfowl and other birds. This juxtaposition of high voltage excitement and the serenity of unspoiled nature is a common occurrence along the Shore, but more so in Atlantic County. The area around Atlantic City is congested, noisy. Out on the Mullica River, you can hear the fish bite. More so than any other county, Atlantic is tourist conscious. Slick brochures promote summer events in and around Atlantic City, and casino gambling brings in people year-round, round the clock. From Brigantine to Margate the oceanfront is lined with high-rise condos and expensive modern mansions. But west of the Garden State Parkway, Atlantic County is delightfully open. The Mullica River has a culture all its own worth exploring, and the roads that run along it take you deep into the Pine Barrens.

Chestnut Neck Battle Monument

Route 9
Port Republic

DIRECTIONS: Take the Garden State Parkway to Exit 48, to Route 9 south. The monument is up ahead on the left, a 50-foot pillar topped by a Colonial soldier.

Ask New Jerseyans about Revolutionary War history in their state, and they'll tell you about Washington's hard winter at Jockey Hollow, or the Christmas attack at Trenton, or the Battle of Monmouth on a blistering hot day that made a folk hero out of Molly Pitcher. The more knowledgeable may tell you about Washington's spying activities in the Watchung Mountains, or Benedict Arnold's trial for treason in Morristown, or that Washington wrote his farewell to arms in a farmhouse at Rocky Hill.

But the battle of Chestnut Neck wouldn't make many lists. Too bad, because this one had all the elements of a classic: revenge . . . intrigue . . . pirates . . . spies . . . sailing warships and fast frigates . . . a rescue force that arrives just *past* the nick of time.

During the Revolution, Britain maintained her trade with the colonies, and the route between New York and Philadelphia, along the Jersey coasts, was as busy as ever.

Some enterprising American boat captains along the Jersey Shore saw some profit in this. War was on, the rules were off. The ragged harbors, rivers, and inlets along the coast were perfect for privateers, who could dash out of friendly waters, knock over a British frigate, and escape back. What's more, the big British warships could never sail far up the Mullica River or give adequate chase around the tiny islands in Little Egg Harbor, Great Bay, or Little Bay. The sandbars and shoals in the Brigantine area were hard enough to negotiate for experienced American captains.

In his book *South Jersey Towns—History and Legends* (Rutgers

University Press), author William McMahon writes that a total 452 privateers worked the Barnegat-Brigantine area from 1776 to 1782. Chestnut Neck, upriver on the Mullica, was a main privateer safe haven, along with Toms River, inland on the Toms River, and Mays Landing, inland on the Great Egg Harbor River.

A group of privateers commandeered two British merchant ship off Sandy Hook in the summer of 1778 and were escorted back to Chestnut Neck. The privateers were brazen enough to advertise the auction of the ship contents in a Pennsylvania newspaper. Not surprisingly, the notice got the attention of the British. In late September, a fleet of nine British warships left New York for Little Egg Harbor. On board were about five hundred foot-soldiers, including the hundred-man 3d Battalion New Jersey Volunteers, a fighting force of British loyalists.

Colonial spies found out about the plan and relayed the information to Washington, who dispatched Gen. Casimir Pulaski and his mounted regiment to Chestnut Neck from Red Bank.

The British convoy was hampered by bad winds. They passed Sandy Hook on September 30th, but did not arrive in Little Egg Harbor until October 6th. The fleet, under the direction of Capt. Henry Collins, planned to wait for good winds to whisk them into the harbor, but British loyalist spies got word to them that Pulaski was on the way. Collins ordered the troops ashore. A small group of American volunteers was waiting for them, and fired from the marshes as the British soldiers approached, but they could not repel the attack. Once on shore, the well-trained British regulars and New Jersey Tories drove the Colonists back. The village of Chestnut Neck was unprotected, and the British burned it to the ground. They also burned about a dozen boats at the Chestnut Neck wharf, the town tavern, and warehouse. The British then ventured up Bass River and burned a sawmill, a saltworks, and twelve homes before returning to their ships. Pulaski arrived two days later. A detachment of his troops was ambushed, and forty-four men were killed less than a week later at Tuckerton by the same British forces that burned Chestnut Neck. Once again, Pulaski arrived at the battle scene after the battle.

The fifty-foot high monument is in a small triangular roadside park off Route 9. It is topped by a Colonial soldier looking east over the harbor and has a plaque below that says: In Honor of the Brave Patriots of the Revolutionary War who Defended Their Liberties and Their Homes in a Battle Fought Near This Site on Oct. 6, 1778. The monument was dedicated on October 6, 1911, the one hundred and thirty-third anniversary of the battle.

Nearby is a small piece of rough sandstone with a bronze plaque that pays tribute to the privateers and their ships, with names like Baker Hendrick and his ship *Charming Betsey,* Teunis Vorhees and *Revenge,* and the Willits brothers, Amos and Enoch, and their ships *Hope* and *Luck & Fortune.*

Marine Mammal Stranding Center Museum

> Brigantine Boulevard
> Brigantine
> (609) 266-0538

OPEN: From Memorial Day to Labor Day, daily: 11 A.M. to 5 P.M. Off-season hours are Saturdays and Sundays: NOON to 4 P.M.

COST: Donations accepted.

DIRECTIONS: Take Route 30 East to Route 87 (also 187) north. (Or once in Atlantic City, follow signs to Trump Castle and Harrah's.) Follow road over the Brigantine Bridge onto Brigantine Boulevard. The Stranding Center is 2 miles up on the left.

Like any first aid squad, the people at the Marine Mammal Stranding Center can be called upon at any time of the day or night to help a sea animal in distress, or, unhappily, to retrieve the remains.

The Center, started in 1978 with a small group of volunteers, is part of the Northeast Stranding network. Rescue workers from Brigantine can be dispatched to help turn around a dolphin in the Shrewsbury River, or sent down along the Delmarva coast to unbeach a humpback whale. Anywhere there's a sea mammal in trouble along the Jersey coast or other eastern states, volunteers from the Marine Mammal Stranding Center will go to help. The Center rescuers have taken part in close to twelve hundred operations, saving whales, dolphins, sea turtles, seals, and other sea animals.

Public access to the Stranding Center's sea animal hospital is somewhat restricted. Sometimes, there are no animals. Other times, the animal may be so critical, the staff will declare keep the Center off limits. If staffers are busy with a rescue or with nursing an animal, the public can only interfere. If the staff is not busy, they may give a brief tour of the facility, but visitors to the Center shouldn't count on being shown the inside.

The Center's museum, however, is always open. The museum explains the Stranding Center's mission and has photographs of some rescues, including the unbeaching of a twenty-five ton humpback whale in Ocean City, Maryland.

Suspended from the ceiling of the museum are fiberglass casts of actual exotic fish and sea mammals recovered by the center. It is a rainbow of giant sea-creature colors: the rusty brown thrasher shark, the deep blue mako, and gray hammerhead sharks, the orange and silver moonfish, the yellow and blue-speckled dolphin fish, the greenish gray of the giant mola.

They are not the only exotic sea life that can be seen at the museum. Out back, there is a thousand-gallon fish tank which holds hundreds of species of sea life found off the Jersey Shore.

"There's so much more to see back there. The kids like it much better because the fish are alive," said Ilona Boyle, the museum manager. "It really hold their interest and adults, too."

Kids can peer into the water with glass bottom containers to get a fish's-eye view of the fish. The first thing they learn is that you don't have to travel to the tropics to see weird and colorful fish dodging around in shallow water off the coast. They're right here in New Jersey.

The second thing they learn is that weird fish usually have weird names: the horse-eyed jack, the three-spine stickleback, the mummichog, the boring sponge (as opposed to the exciting sponge?), and the needlefish are just a few of the local species that look as weird as they sound.

Brigantine Historical Museum

> 3607 Brigantine Boulevard
> Brigantine
> (609) 266-9339

OPEN: Mid-June to the end of September, Saturdays and Sundays: 10 A.M. to 3 P.M. Also by special appointment.

NOTE: The above phone number is disconnected from October to May. Museum staff can be reached by calling (609) 266-3437, which is the Brigantine Chamber of Commerce.

COST: Donations accepted.

DIRECTIONS: Take Route 30 east to Route 87 (also 187) north. Take bridge to Brigantine and continue straight (the street name now becomes Brigantine Boulevard). The museum is 1 block south of the lighthouse, right next door to the Stranding Center.

Lenni-Lenape Indians spent their summers on the island. New England whalers came to the island around 1640, chasing the whales who were running south. Legend has it that

Captain Kidd buried a chest of pirated treasure on the island in the summer of 1698. It has never been found.

This is just part of Brigantine's colorful and crazy history. Pirates hid there. Revolutionary War sea battles were fought there. It was under threat of pillage by the British in the War of 1812.

Then things got really wild. As early as 1828, Brigantine had a small summer trade, starting with the Holscomb House, which burned down in 1851, was rebuilt and burned down again in 1903. But the first big explosion in Brigantine development came in the late 1880s.

"Everything was built up on the north end of the island . . . that's where all the activity was," said Dolly Simpson of the Brigantine Historical Society.

Hotels were built. A trolley service developed. Seaside cottages were constructed. It was the epitome of Victorian seaside living, akin to summer life at Ocean Grove or Cape May. And it's all gone. Like the lost continent of Atlantis, old Brigantine is under water.

"The town ended around 51st Street. Now it ends around 14th," Simpson said.

And while Captain Kidd's sunken treasure hasn't been found, the Brigantine Historical Society Museum has an entire collection of treasures from old Brigantine that have washed up in the surf.

"We have a display of just things that people have found on the beach: dishes from Holland House—which washed away in 1912—silverware, cannon balls from the Revolution, pieces of the trolley tracks," said Rose Arnold, the secretary of the historical society. "We even have some of the ships' logs from some of the ships that have wrecked here."

And there have been plenty of them. More than three hundred ships have beached and broken up or sunk on the shoals of Brigantine, the last being a fishing vessel in 1992; her mast juts out of the ocean at the north end of the island.

Hurricanes and nor'easters have been the main culprit in north Brigantine's disappearance. The home of James Baremore, Brigantine's first year-round resident was washed away in a big storm in 1830, having survived repeated attempts by the sea to claim it after it was built in 1802.

The Holland House was lost to a storm in 1912.

The United States Lifesaving Service Station building, built in 1846, survived 98 years before the hurricane of 1944 put it under.

"We had big storms in 1939, '44, '60, '61 and '63," said Rose Arnold. Each time, a little more of the town disappeared.

The nor'easter of '93, however, had the reverse effect. For the first time in almost fifty years, the foundation of the Lifesaving Service Station reappeared on the Brigantine beach.

The museum, which doubles as the town's tourist center, is set up like a chronological walk through Brigantine history, including a room devoted to the Lenni-Lenape Indians.

Most of the artifacts are photos from the extensive collection of the late Fritz Haneman, whose grandfather, John Harris, helped develop the town in its second land boom, in the 1920s. It was Harris who, in 1927, built the nonfunctioning lighthouse, which still stands in the middle of Roosevelt Boulevard as a real estate sales gimmick.

Photos include the original giant hotels—the Holscomb, the Holland and the Smith, which was on the site where the Brigantine Hotel (now a condo association) was built in 1926—and of many seaside cottages that were eventually washed away. There's a photo of the lighthouse, which now sits at a congested town center, with nothing around it. For awhile, the lighthouse held the town jail, and the door to the slammer is on display at the museum, as well as photos of the original lock-up.

There are also photos of the beleaguered Brigantine Bridge. First built in 1924, the bridge was washed away in 1938 and again in 1944. Twenty-five years of ocean pounding made the bridge unsafe, and it was condemned in 1969. The current span, completed in 1972, goes high above the waves and seems to be holding up okay.

One of the highlights of the museum is a three-foot wooden model of the U.S.S. *New Jersey,* built by John Clark of Brigantine. Mr. Clark has apparently made models of every major ship in the U.S. fleet and recently donated fifty models to the U.S. Naval Academy in Annapolis, Maryland.

Absecon Lighthouse

>   Pacific and Rhode Island Avenues
>   Atlantic City

OPEN: Closed until future renovation is complete.

DIRECTIONS: From the Atlantic City Expressway entrance into Atlantic City, go straight to Pacific Avenue and make a left. The lighthouse is 17 blocks ahead on the left. While the lighthouse is no longer the tallest structure in town, having been topped by a number of high-rise casino-hotels, it does tower over its immediate neighborhood. You can't miss it.

As early as 1695, the small harbor in what today is north Atlantic City was known as Graveyard Inlet, one of the most treacherous stretches of coast along the Atlantic seaboard.

By the time Jonathan Pitney, the Mendham doctor who relocated to Atlantic County in 1820, discovered the inlet, it was known as Absecon Beach. Pitney, who believed in the recuperative powers of salt air and sea, was known to send patients to the tiny village at the inlet's edge as part of their treatment.

Pitney, however, was alarmed at the loss of life and cargo at the inlet. He knew the cure: a lighthouse. He researched old wrecks and kept records of the new ones. In the early 1840s, after years of lobbying by Dr. Pitney, the Navy Department decided to study his proposal for a lighthouse. Then they decided against it.

By now Pitney had helped turn Absecon Beach into a popular little resort. The Camden and Atlantic Railroad came in June of 1852; less than two years later Absecon Beach was incorporated as a city—Atlantic City.

As the city grew, trade increased. And so did shipping losses due to wrecks. Pitney continued to push for the lighthouse, this time lobbying Congress. In 1854 Congress appropriated thirty-five thousand dollars to build the Absecon Lighthouse.

On January 15, 1857, the lighthouse was complete. It was 170-feet high and made from almost 600,000 bricks. The lighthouse's 36-plate Fresnel lens, powered by about three gallons of oil a day, threw a beam 19½ miles out from the coastline. Its bright white light bleached the darkness out of the harbor and its shipwreck reputation began to fade.

The Absecon Light in Victorian times. Princeton Antiques Bookshop, Atlantic City.

Shifting sands alert! When the lighthouse was built, it was judged to be seven hundred feet from shoreline during high tide. An 1877 map of the Atlantic City includes the 1852 shoreline survey, which shows the ocean about seven hundred feet in either direction from where the lighthouse was to be built. By 1877, according to the same map, the waves were breaking less than a block away, and some surrounding streets were under water. Now the light stands in the middle of a neighborhood—fifteen hundred feet from the nearest water.

The light went electric in 1925, but the most frequent changes in the lighthouse were the color schemes. It's original brick façade was changed to red and white, then to black and orange during the early part of the twentieth century. It became blue and white, Atlantic City's colors, then back to red and white in the 1980s. It remains that way today, except for the graffiti spray-painted around it's base.

The lighthouse was decommissioned in 1933. It was scheduled to be taken down in 1946, but a public outcry saved it, but not the lightkeepers house, which was demolished.

The light was lit one last time, at midnight on December 31, 1963, to kick off New Jersey's Tercentennial celebration. Seven years later, the lighthouse, which belongs to the state Division of Parks and Forestry, was placed on the State Register of Historic Places. A year later, it made the national list. The light-house's historical designation, assured that it would be saved from the wrecking ball, but did little to protect it from vandals.

As a target for vandals in a deteriorating neighborhood, the lighthouse was under constant attack. Graffiti went up as high as a spray-painter's arm could reach. The grounds around it were littered with broken bottles. It almost seemed as if the miscreants who lived near the lighthouse would achieve what one hundred and thirty years of Mother Nature's worst nights could not do.

In 1988, the lighthouse got another boost from Atlantic City

The Absecon Light today. Note how the neighborhood has changed. Courtesy of
The Star-Ledger.

residents. The Inlet Public Private Association (IPPA), the group trying to restore and revitalize the inlet area, made the Absecon Lighthouse their official logo. It was not only acknowledgment that the lighthouse is the most important remaining structure in the area, but a constant reminder that the old beacon is still a symbol of hope for a vessel trying to find it's way. In this case, the vessel is the IPPA, bringing back a downtrodden neighborhood.

In 1993 the IPPA decided to renovate and reopen the lighthouse. A museum and gift shop may be part of the package. While funding and plans are incomplete, the lighthouse restoration is an important part of the IPPA's master plan for Absecon Beach, which will include shops, restaurants, and a wharf area all designed to bring some tourism money out of the casinos and into the north end. And if that happens, the lighthouse may again be the beacon that throws a light over Graveyard Inlet.

The Atlantic City Historical Museum

Garden Pier
Boardwalk and New Jersey Avenue
Atlantic City
(609) 347-5837

OPEN: Daily: 10 A.M. to 4 P.M., except major holidays in the off-season.

COST: Free.

DIRECTIONS: From the Atlantic City Expressway entrance into Atlantic City, go straight to Pacific Avenue. Make a left on Pacific and head north 14 blocks to New Jersey Avenue. Make a right and go to the boardwalk. There is a free parking lot for Garden Pier visitors next to the boardwalk. The historical museum is the building on the right-hand side of the Garden Pier complex.

🦚   Casinos, high-rise hotels and condominiums, chain restaurants, and stores dominate the boardwalk. There's a Planet Hollywood at Caesars, a Warner Bros. Studio at Trumps. There's Burger King and McDonalds, and the same Italian fast-food place you see at Parkway reststops.

While there are still a large number of souvenir shops, arcades, fortune tellers, salt-water taffy and peanut places on the boardwalk, it's obvious that the boardwalk has been moving more commercially mainstream since the advent of casino gambling.

But don't worry. There's still plenty of old Atlantic City to be found, if you know where to look.

For instance, the terra cotta façade of the Warner movie theater—a Spanish-Moorish architectural gem with bronze doors, gold trimmed mirrors, luxurious seats and carpets, and a marble lobby—still stands on the boardwalk just north of Caesars. The façade is chipped and faded, and it towers over a karaoke snack bar, but enough remains to see the ghost of its grandeur.

The boardwalk today on a fall afternoon in 1994.

Warner Theater facade in 1995—all that's left of what was once the world's most ornate movie theater.

You can see a number of historical structures that have survived the casino steamroller, but the best place to start is the
Atlantic City Historical Museum at Garden Pier. This is old
Atlantic City. Visitors here are greeted by the Mr. Peanut who
stood outside the Planters Peanut store at Virginia Avenue and
Boardwalk as early as 1916. On the other side of Mr. Peanut is
a large quotation from Theodore Roosevelt. "A man would not
be a good American citizen if he did not know of Atlantic City."

The museum has another sign near the entrance. "Atlantic
City—Playground of the Nation." The museum then goes on
to back that claim up with a wonderful collection of photographs and memorabilia and a thirty-five minute video called
Boardwalk Ballyhoo.

Let's start with Mr. Peanut. Everyone knows Mr. Peanut . . .
he is still plastered on Planters cans, and it was the Atlantic
City boardwalk that made Mr. Peanut an American trademark
icon. Millions of visitors a year would pass Mr. Peanut on the
boardwalk and—in the days before electronic media—that was
the best advertising money could buy. Planters parlayed Mr.
Peanut's popularity into gift shop sales. Along with a half-pound
of dry roasted peanuts or salted cashews, boardwalk customers
could come away with Mr. Peanut dishes, Mr. Peanut salt and
pepper shakers, Mr. Peanut drink stirrers, Mr. Peanut cups—
all of which are on display in the museum.

Mr. Peanut, distinguished in his top hat and monocle, is a
symbol of the national commercial power the Atlantic City
boardwalk held back when top hats and monocles were worn
by gentlemen.

When Goodyear made the world's biggest tire, they rolled
it down the boardwalk. When Underwood made the world's
biggest typewriter with each key the size of a child-sized bar
stool, they brought it to the boardwalk. When Dr. Martin A.
Couney wanted to make a case for the infant incubator, which
he claimed to invent, he brought it to the boardwalk. For parts

of four decades, Couney had a season-long exhibit of premature babies living in incubators on the boardwalk. Gawkers paid a quarter, to help offset the cost of the infants' care.

That was Atlantic City. Tacky. Bizarre. Free-wheeling. And sexy. And this was long, long, long before the casinos. It was a place where fads began, where public tastes were gauged and their tolerance tested. It was P.T. Barnum's museum rolled out like a wooden carpet along a two-mile stretch of sand, and people couldn't resist it. Where else could you find Professor Nelson's Boxing Cats or the High Diving Horses? Or the Flying Zachinis, who were fired out of cannons? Or the falling Joseph Hackney, who jumped into the sea from a blimp 145 feet in the air? Miss America? How about Miss Chambermaid, the winner of an annual bed-making contest in a boardwalk event that could only be described as an Olympics for hotel staffs, as waiters raced up and down the planks with trays filled with food.

The boardwalk was empty in the off-season until casino gambling arrived. Princeton Antiques Bookshop, Atlantic City.

That was Atlantic City. It was big, loud, lightbulb bright, and neon colorful. For three months a year, it was the city that never slept, the entertainment capital of the world. In the book *Atlantic City: 125 years of Ocean Madness* by Vicki Gold Levi and Lee Eisenberg (Ten Speed Press) there is this quote from a 1915 magazine article by James Huneker:

"Atlantic City is not a treat for the introspective. It is all on the surface; it is hard, glittering, unspeakably cacophonous, and it never sleeps at all. Three days and you crave the comparative solitude of Broadway and Thirty-fourth Street; a week and you may die of insomnia."

The museum captures that spirit. There is a wall devoted to the stars, the biggest names in American pop culture, who played there. There is a wall devoted to the movies made there. Of course, there is a Miss America wall, and a wall devoted to the luxury hotels. There are pictures of the Steel Pier and turn-of-century contraptions called mechanical rides that tilted and whirled or jostled and hoisted enough to thrill but, usually,

Rolling-chair pusher Arthur W. Hill. The chair pushers are a remnant of old Atlantic City. Courtesy of The Star-Ledger.

brought every one back in one piece. There are pictures of people being pushed in rolling chairs, a century-old tradition. There are pictures of the sand artists at work in front of crowds of thousands.

And all these pictures have one thing in common: everybody is always smiling.

Some of the sand-sculpture gargoyles and other heads and figures are on display in the museum because the sand used in these figures are mixed with concrete to give it form and endurance. The sand sculptures on display belong to Robert Ruffolo (see Princeton Books) who obtained them after they were extracted from deep in the beach sand, decades after they were made. The artists lived only on the generosity of the boardwalk crowd, who threw coins down on the beach to show their appreciation.

Outside the museum in the fountain area are a number of gargoyles and animals sculptures that decorated the Marlborough-Blenheim Hotel, which was one of the first major buildings anywhere to built out of Thomas Edison's reinforced cement. Edison himself supervised the project. In 1906 this was a milestone along the Jersey Shore, where wind-whipped fires had run through rambling, wooden Victorian hotels from Long Branch to Cape May, sometimes wiping out blocks of resort buildings. Now here was Thomas Edison with a fireproof hotel.

Italian artists were brought to America to craft the ceramic sculptures that adorned the hotel, which looked like an elaborate and exotic Mosque. Sea eagles nested in upper towers and on top of the dome; sea turtles and sea horses and dolphins and fish frolicked on columns. There were shells everywhere.

When the building came down in 1979, the gargoyles were plucked out of the rubble by preservationists led by Florence Valore Miller, executive director of the Atlantic City museum. Some of the survivors are on display on the boardwalk . . . right where they belong.

Princeton Books

2915 Atlantic Avenue
Atlantic City
(609) 344-1943

OPEN: Monday through Friday: 8 A.M. to 5 P.M.; Saturdays: 8 A.M. to 1 P.M. Closed Sundays.

COST: Free to browse

DIRECTIONS: Princeton Books is on Atlantic Avenue, south of the Atlantic City Expressway entrance to town. The building takes up most of the block, and the sign is enormous, so it's hard to miss.

All day, people come in off the street with things to sell Robert Eugene Ruffolo, the owner of Princeton Books. Ruffolo, who deals in rare and out-of-print books and other antiques, is a tough sell. He doesn't always want someone else's junk.

"I got enough of my own," he says.

But when it comes to Atlantic City memorabilia, Ruffolo is a soft sell. He can't get enough of it. In fact, he has two collections: the commercial collection, which is for sale at Princeton Books, and his personal collection, which will remain personal, except for the items he has loaned to the Atlantic City Historical Museum.

Ruffolo, the chairman of the museum, has Atlantic City memorabilia in nearly every corner of his home. At Princeton Books, which has department store-sized frontage along Atlantic Avenue, Ruffolo devotes half a room to Atlantic City. It's safe to say he has the greatest Atlantic City paper-memorabilia collection in the world. He has over twenty thousand postcards, in forty-some binders that hold five hundred postcards apiece. He has one hundred binders of Atlantic City photographs. The walls of the section are decorated with advertising signs, art prints, and posters of Atlantic City landmarks and boardwalk scenes. Ruffolo has a collection of illustrations from publications like *Harpers Weekly*, including drawings of the destruction following the storm of 1884 and one of a Victorian age contraption called the Ocean Tricycle, which took people for an off-road ride in the surf.

Ruffolo has other souvenir memorabilia, like a collection of salt-water taffy boxes, plates, banks, paperweights, even casino chips. Ruffolo's sand-art collection from the 1940s, is on permanent display at the Atlantic City Historical Museum.

"To me, (Atlantic City) always has been a fascinating subject," Ruffolo said of his town. "Everybody all over the world has heard of this place. It's one of the most famous places in world, and yet so many little pieces of it are just gone. I guess what I do is to preserve those little pieces, so somebody down the line will be able to put them together and get an idea of the way things used to be here."

Somers Mansion

> 1000 Shore Road (on circle near MacArthur Boulevard)
> Somers Point
> (609) 927-2212

OPEN: Wednesday through Saturday: 10 A.M. to 5 P.M. Sundays: 1 P.M. to 5 P.M. Closed most major holidays during the winter.

COST: Free

DIRECTIONS: Take Exit 30 south from the Garden State Parkway to Route 52, which is also named MacArthur Boulevard. Cross over Route 9. Just before the circle, look for the driveway to the Somers Mansion on the left.

Some historians think the Somers Mansion was built by John Somers in 1714. Other think it was built in the 1720s by Richard Somers, one of John Somers's ten children. Either way, the Somers Mansion dates back to the earliest days of Atlantic

County's First Family. The mansion itself is the oldest intact house in the county and only one of two county homes to be included on the National Register of Historic Places. The other is the Risley Homestead at 8 Virginia Avenue in Northfield, a two-hundred-and-seventy-year-old plain farm house that was home to twenty generations of oystermen. Call (609) 641-8976.

John Somers, an English Quaker, came to Atlantic County by way of Pennsylvania. In March of 1693 Somers acquired the deed to three thousand acres along the Great Egg Bay, which became known as Somers Plantation before evolving into Somers Point.

The same month, he was appointed "supervisor of roads and constable for Great Egg Harbor," by the Cape May County "Court of Portsmouth."

Two years later, John Somers began a ferry across Great Egg Bay, linking his plantation and the surrounding areas with Cape May County.

The ferry master was Job Somer's, and the launch area became known as Job's Point.

The Somers Mansion is a fairly plain Dutch Colonial house; the most interesting part is the roof. The roof is constructed like the hull of a ship, but upside down.

The house is most famous for being the birthplace of Commodore Richard Somers, the great-grandson of John Somers. It was this Richard Somers who brought fame to the town named after his family and glory to the family name (see following item).

Atlantic County Historical Museum

907 Shore Road
Somers Point
(609) 927-5218

OPEN: Wednesday through Saturday: 10 A.M. to 3:30 P.M.

COST: Donations accepted.

DIRECTIONS: Take Exit 30 south from Garden State Park-way. Take Route 52 east (also MacArthur Boulevard) to the circle. Go three-quarters of the way around and head north on Shore Road (also Route 585). The mu-seum is ¼ mile up on the left. To get to the parking lot, take the first left off Shore Road, which is Somers Av-enue, then a quick left on Centre Street. Centre Street dead-ends at the back door (the main entrance) of the museum.

The upstairs floor of the Atlantic County Histori-cal Museum is called the nautical room, and one corner of it is devoted to Commodore Richard Somers, the town's authentic war hero and great-grandson of town founder John Somers.

Richard Somers is not some obscure figure in American military history being promoted by his little town. In fact, a monument to his bravery now stands at the Naval Academy in Annapolis, having been moved there from the old Washing-ton, D.C., Navy Yard in 1860. And the most enduring tribute to Somers is the U.S. Navy's continued penchant for naming ships after him. Since his death in 1804 "on the shores of Tri-poli," six U.S. Navy ships have carried the name U.S.S. *Somers.*

Pictures of all six are displayed at the museum. The mu-seum also has a collection of intricate model ships made by a later descendent, Hubert Somers, including the *Santa Maria,* the *Constitution,* the *Bon Homme Richard,* and the *Somers,* a naval train-ing ship built in 1842.

Richard Somers received an naval officer's commission in 1798 when he was twenty and came aboard the *United States,* one of the U.S. Navy's earliest ships. Six years later, Somers's leg-end was made during the war with the Barbary pirates.

After the ship *Philadelphia* was captured in Tripoli, the crew was taken prisoner, except for a young officer named Stephen Decatur, who burned the frigate before escaping, rendering it useless to the pirates. Decatur was a good friend of Somers, and his daring escape inspired Somers to come up with an equally daring plan to free the *Philadelphia* crew.

Somers loaded a small boat with a hundred barrels of gunpowder, a hundred and fifty mortar rounds, and iron scraps. The idea was to pilot the boat loaded with explosives toward the pirate fleet in Tripoli Harbor, light a long fuse on board, and escape in row boats before the powder exploded and the scrap iron became shrapnel.

Unfortunately the boat exploded prematurely, killing Somers and his crew. His body was never recovered. But word of his plan-gone-awry spread back to the Washington, and Somers gained war-hero status immediately. While the war with the Barbary pirates has been reduced to anecdotal status in American history, in Somers Point, it was the conflict that put the town on the map.

The nautical room of the museum includes the history of another important Atlantic County family, the boat building Van Sants. John Van Sant started a boatyard in the Somers Point region in 1796. For the next 136 years, Van Sants handcrafted schooners and other boat in a variety of Atlantic County locations, including Absecon, Atlantic City, Port Republic, New Gretna, and Tuckerton.

The museum has a wall dedicated to the Van Sant shipbuilders, including a collection of old tools and half models, which were crucial to the building of a full-sized ship.

Longport Historical Museum

> 2305 Atlantic Ave.
> Longport
> (609) 823-1115

OPEN: Memorial Day weekend through the end of September, Saturdays: 9 A.M. to NOON. Museum is also open by appointment (including winter). Call (609) 823-7514, which is the town's municipal building.

COST: Donations accepted.

DIRECTIONS: Atlantic Avenue is the main street in Longport. It can be reached by following Route 152 from Somers Point (near Exits 30 north and 29 south on the Garden State Parkway) over the bridge to Longport, or coming down through Atlantic City, Ventnor, and Margate.

The official documentation of Longport's history only began in the mid-1980s, but luck, and longevity, were on the side of town historian, Michael Cohen, and other organizers of the effort. Cohen was able to interview a number of people who were in Longport almost from the start.

Christian L. Frye, the first person born in the town of Longport, was still alive and living in town. Eleanor McCullough Moore Webster, the granddaughter of town founder Simpson McCullough, was in a Philadelphia-area nursing home. Octogenarian Ed Stetzer, whose father ran a sport fishing boat off the old Longport pier in the early twentieth century, still lived in town, as did Richard DePamphilis, the town's first police chief.

"We have tremendous family continuity here," said Cohen.

Cohen was lucky in another respect. Not only could these people give lucid oral histories of the town, they were all collectors to some degree, and furnished the memorabilia that launched the Longport Historical Museum. Cohen visited Mrs. Webster once a week for months and recorded her memories about the earliest days of Longport. In time she began to donate family items that dealt with Longport history, including a scientific algae study, complete with pressed and dried specimens from the sea off of Longport, that won her grandmother a science bronze medal at the Colombian Exhibition in Chicago in 1892.

Another long-timer, Morris Swope, got behind the history gathering effort and called the other long-timers in town and told them to clean out their attics.

The result is a six-room local museum that touches on every aspect of Longport's development.

When Simon McCullough, a wealthy Philadelphia Quaker, decided he, too, wanted to develop a Jersey Shore town during the oceanfront real-estate bonanza of the 1880s, he went to the southernmost tip of the Abesecon Island, about seven miles below Atlantic City, and found a little barrier island with sand dunes two-stories high.

McCullough's plan was simple: flatten the sand dunes into beautiful wide beaches and begin to build a summer resort.

At the time McCullough came to town, there were only two structures on the island—the farmhouse owned by the Frye family and a U.S. Lifesaving Station, which had been commissioned in 1849, one of the first ten in the nation.

Here's some more local family continuity. Current Longport housing inspector Herb Gaskell, who is in his eighties, had a great-grandfather who was appointed by Abraham Lincoln to serve in the Lifesaving Station on the barren island. The family never left. Gaskell's father served there, too.

McCullough built a little hotel with a restaurant, called the Aberdeen.

"It was like the Pocono land deals they have today," Cohen said. "McCullough would bring people in from Atlantic City, put them up in his hotel. The he would show them the lots for sale. Back then you could get a lot for five hundred dollars or a buy a whole block for three thousand. Today, by comparison, the cheapest oceanfront lot in Longport is worth about a million."

The town began to take shape. Other hotels were built: the Devonshire, which burned down in 1911; the Oberon, which eventually became an exclusive school for boys, enrolling, among others, the heirs to the DuPont company. The building today is the Winchester Hotel.

Another major component in the town's popularity with

wealthy Philadelphians was the Bayview Fishing and Gun Club, which was an extension of the exclusive Union League of Philadelphia. The Bayview closed after World War I and became Majestic Apartments and Hotel, then the Canterbury. Historian Cohen lives there today. More continuity.

A pier was built where steamship ferries from Somers Point and Ocean City could dock. In 1884 the railroad was extended south from Atlantic City into Longport. The tiny resort benefited immensely from the added transportation, especially the railroad. Everything was going according to McCullough's plan. The railroad even supplied the rock wall on the bayside that kept the water from reuniting with the ocean over the island's low point.

But the best laid plans of Simpson McCullough could not stop nature from taking its course. The wide flat beaches, where Louis Chevrolet and other automotive pioneers raced early automobiles, were taking a pounding.

The first boardwalk, built with the help of a young Christian L. Frye, was washed away.

"I asked him once, 'About how wide was the boardwalk,' " Cohen recalled. "He said, 'twelve-feet, two-inches.' I said, 'How can you remember that after all this time,' and he said, 'because I put down every board myself.'"

Longport, which is mostly residential today, with expensive homes lining the beach, shifted from a commercial resort to a single-family home vacation spot in 1914 when the automobile bridge was built from Somers Point.

"Many of the Quaker families had built summer Victorian cottages, and that's just the direction the town took," Cohen said.

The Quakers' Church of the Redeemer doubled as the town hall until 1908 when a new Spanish Mission–style church was built. The world-renowned Willits Company of Philadelphia, which did the stained-glass windows at Princeton University and the American Cathedral in Washington, did the windows for the new church. The church, at 20th and Atlantic Avenues, is on the National Register of Historic Places.

The museum's first room houses the Webster-McCullough collection, and pictures of the Frye family farm. The second room holds picture albums and memorabilia from the old hotels, the railroad, and pier. In addition to the steamship ferries, there were fishing boats and other pleasure crafts docked at the pier, including Ed Stetzer's father's boat, the *Polly Page Two*. There is also an exhibit about the construction of the massive twenty-four-hundred-foot long sea wall, which was built between 1917 and 1920. The wall, which still stands, has kept Longport beaches from washing away in this century. There are also storm pictures, including the storm of 1944, which washed away Longport's second—and final—boardwalk, and the March storm of '62.

"That was the worst one," Cohen said. "That was a five-high-tide storm, it lasted two and a half days. We got flooding from the ocean and bay, and fifteen homes were lost." (A "five-high-tide storm" is one that lasts through five high tides of which there are two daily, making a five-high-tide storm one that lasts two and a half days.)

The third room is built around Richard DePamphilis's collection. DePamphilis was police chief between 1931 and 1974 and was succeeded, first, by his son, and then, by two nephews. The exhibit features a two-way police radio that belonged to the department, only the third in the nation to be used back in the 1930s.

Another room holds the Betty Bacharach Home exhibit. Mrs. Bacharach, aunt of composer Burt Bacharach, started a home for children with infantile paralysis in Longport in the early 1920s. The exhibit features medical equipment, such as electrical stimulators, that were used on the children, and a collection of photos of celebrities who came to the home to visit the children and perform in fund-raisers, including Bob Hope, Betty Grable, Ronald Reagan, Stan Laurel and Oliver Hardy, and Sarah Delano Roosevelt, the mother of FDR.

The lifeguard and Coast Guard exhibit includes the expected, such as lifeguard surfboards, and the unexpected, like bottles of Canadian Whiskey that were dumped overboard by rumrunners during Prohibition.

"I don't think Atlantic City suffered too much during Prohibition," Cohen said. "The alcohol was coming in through the inlets on the island. When the Coast Guard would go out to these boats, they would dump their cargo overboard. The bottles still wash up from time to time."

Lucy the Margate Elephant

Atlantic and Decatur Avenues
Margate
(609) 823-6473

OPEN: Mid-June to Labor Day, daily: 10 A.M. to 8 P.M. Spring and fall, weekends only: 10 A.M. to 4:30 P.M. Closed November through March.

COST: $2 for adults, $1 for children.

DIRECTIONS: Take the Garden State Parkway to Exit 36. Take Tilton Road east, which becomes the Margate Bridge Road, which becomes Jerome Avenue in Margate. Cross over Ventnor Avenue to Atlantic Avenue, which parallels the beach. Turn right on Atlantic. Lucy is about ¼ mile down on the left.

Sandwiched between two high-rise condo buildings on the Margate beachfront is a hefty slice of Jerseyana. She's Lucy the Margate Elephant, the heavyweight champ of New Jersey roadside attractions. Visitors to Lucy can climb to the observation deck of her howdah and get a lighthouse-like view of the ocean. Inside, Lucy offers a minihistorical museum, with

Lucy the Margate Elephant.

pictures and artifacts of old Margate and old Lucy. After all, the two are directly linked.

In Margate, where all road signs lead to Lucy, she's not only the town's most famous resident—she's a National Historical Landmark—but its oldest, too. In fact, Lucy, who was built in 1881, predates the town name of Margate by nearly thirty years. From 1885 to 1897 Margate was known as Borough of South Atlantic City, then it was renamed the City of South Atlantic City. The name Margate was adopted in 1909.

Lucy was built in 1881, a time when many existing shore towns were experiencing a burst of popularity and land speculators rushed in to capitalize on vacant oceanfront properties.

James V. Lafferty, an engineer and inventor, saw a chance to move some of the lots he owned in South Atlantic City, but he needed a way to draw people away from the bright lights and ballyhoo of the Atlantic City boardwalk.

In those days, Atlantic City was booming, and South Atlantic City was barren. Lafferty needed a gimmick. A big gimmick.

He designed a colossal elephant and paid thirty-eight thousand dollars to have it built. Lafferty knew people would come to see the elephant and, once in town, there was a chance he could persuade them to purchase some oceanfront property.

Lafferty was right. People came. Lucy was such a big hit, Lafferty had his blueprints patented and built two more—one at Cape May and the other at Coney Island.

The Cape May elephant, called the Light of Asia, went up in 1884. It was only forty feet high—twenty-five feet shorter than the sixty-five-foot Lucy, and not much of a novelty, since a bigger elephant was on the beach in just the next county. The Cape May elephant was a money loser and was torn down in 1900. The Coney Island elephant, called Elephantine Colossus, was one hundred twenty-two feet high, nearly twice the size of Lucy, and was billed as the Eighth Wonder of the World. Also built in 1884, Colossus was a big hit with New Yorkers, but never turned a profit. By the 1890s, the novelty had worn off, and the elephant became a boarding house, fell into disrepair, and was deserted. A fire destroyed it on the night of September 2, 1896.

Unfortunately for Lafferty, his oceanfront lots weren't as big a hit as Lucy, and by 1887, he was forced to sell his property and his elephant.

The buyer was Anthony Gertzen. Lucy would belong to the Gertzen family for the next eighty-three years. Gertzen, who had a number of shore properties and businesses, kept Lucy open as a tourist attraction until his death in 1902. His widow sold the elephant to their son, John. (It was John Gertzen's wife, Sophia, who was credited with naming the elephant Lucy). Part of the package included the Turkish Pavilion, the ornate building Anthony Gertzen had bought and imported from Philadelphia, where it had been part of the 1876 Centennial Celebration. The Turkish Pavilion was set up right behind Lucy, and the Gertzens later bought a nearby hotel. Now Lucy was the centerpiece of Margate nightlife as the Gertzens operated a gambling casino in the hotel and a nightclub in the Pavilion. Business names were the Elephant Hotel and, later, the Elephant Cafe.

Lucy made her first move in 1903, after a hurricane battered the coast and left her buried in sand up to her knees. Volunteers dug her out, then moved her about one hundred feet back from the ocean. The Gertzens turned Lucy into a bar, but after a 1904 fire, decided that drunken crowds were more hazardous to her health than anything Mother Nature could whip up.

John Gertzen died in 1916, leaving his widow, Sophia, with two small children and Lucy. For a while Sophia turned the Lucy beachfront into a tent campgrounds for vacationers. She converted the Turkish Pavilion into a boarding house. Lucy remained a tourist attraction, and for ten cents, visitors could walk through the elephant and peer through any of its twenty-two windows. She remained the main attraction of Sophia Gertzen's seaside businesses until 1963 when Sophia died at age eighty-six. Her children ran the businesses until 1970, then sold everything but Lucy to developers. Lucy was donated to the town.

Lucy had survived the most brutal storms of the century, including those in '44 and '50 in which many homes and other oceanfront buildings were swept away, but the biggest threat to her existence came from developers. Ironic, isn't it? This elephant came into existence to build interest in Margate nearly a century ago. She did her job, and now the people profiting the most from her early work wanted to tear her down.

Fair or not, the developers were closing in on Lucy, and Lucy was an easy target. She was not only in the way, she was also decaying. A Margate civic group, which would later become the Save Lucy Committee, began to raise money to have the elephant moved to a city-owned oceanfront park and restore her. The city gave permission for the project, but on condition that should the elephant have crumbled en route, the committee would be responsible for carting away her remains. The group had to overcome one unexpected obstacle: a company that owned developable property near Lucy's new home sued to keep the elephant off their block, saying she would devalue the property. Lucy won in court.

On July 20, 1970, Lucy made her two-block trip downtown, propped up by heavy wooden scaffolding, placed on a custom-made dolleys and pulled by a semi. Police were on hand to keep the crowds back and power company crews dropped lines along the route to accommodate the rolling pachyderm.

Lucy was placed on her new site, and a hundred and twenty-four thousand dollar restoration was good enough to re-open her for tours in 1974, but left her in far from pristine condition.

The committee applied for more federal and state grant

money, raised more money, and found benefactors such as Irenee DuPont, Jr., who donated the elaborate fire suppression system that was installed in the elephant.

The Save Lucy Committee, led by charter member Josephine Herron, is still fighting to keep Lucy alive. From the outside, the elephant looks beautiful in her new gray suit of sheet-metal. But there is more work to be done to the interior, which has suffered additional deterioration since the 1970s work. The Save Lucy Committee raises money through a snack bar and gift shop, which sells Lucy sweatshirts, T-shirts, pewter magnets, shot glasses, pewter sculptures, blue bottles, and cards.

Cape May County

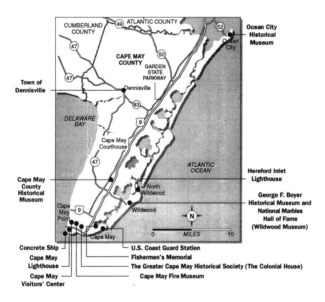

CUMBERLAND COUNTY

ATLANTIC COUNTY

49

47

CAPE MAY COUNTY

50

GARDEN STATE PARKWAY

52

Ocean City

Ocean City Historical Museum

Town of Dennisville

47

Dennisville

83

DELAWARE BAY

9

Cape May Courthouse

47

ATLANTIC OCEAN

Hereford Inlet Lighthouse

Cape May County Historical Museum

North Wildwood

George F. Boyer Historical Museum and National Marbles Hall of Fame (Wildwood Museum)

Cape May Point

9

Wildwood

N

0   MILES   10

Cape May

Concrete Ship

Cape May Lighthouse

Cape May Visitors' Center

U.S. Coast Guard Station

Fishermen's Memorial

The Greater Cape May Historical Society (The Colonial House)

Cape May Fire Museum

In the movie *Dad* the character played by Jack Lemmon is a California aerospace worker who had an ongoing delusional daydream of being a farmer in Cape May, New Jersey. The movie opens with an idyllic scene of a farmer plowing a field, silhouetted by a brilliant sunrise. For people familiar only with Cape May City, this may have looked like a weird image. But the New Jersey cape, like many areas of the state, has rich soil and a long agricultural history. While Cape May was originally settled by whaling families, these yeoman whalers eventually expanded their empires to include plantationlike farms throughout the cape. Even today towns like Rio Grande are major produce centers. Another little known fact about Cape May County, which encompasses the southernmost tip of the state, is exactly how far south it is! Stand on the boardwalk at Cape May and you are farther south than Wheeling, West Virginia; Covington, Kentucky; and Winchester, Virginia. With its stately Victorian ambiance, crowded Cape May City is unique in the county. While there are fine homes in places like Dennisville and Cape May Courthouse, most of the cape is filled with modest homes in small towns. Some places on the Delaware Bay side are downright desolate. Reeds Beach is a point at the end of a sand and stone road, marked by a few house trailers and fishing shacks on stilts. The bay, with its tremendous tidal surges, actually laps up underneath some homes during high tide. It's hard to believe that just a few miles away is one of the nation's premiere seaside resorts.

Ocean City Historical Museum

17th Street and Simpson Avenue
Ocean City
(609) 399-1801

OPEN: Summers, Monday through Friday: 10 A.M. to 4 P.M. and Saturdays: 1 P.M. to 4 P.M. Winters, Tuesday through Saturday: NOON to 3 P.M.

COST: Donations accepted.

DIRECTIONS: Take the Garden State Parkway to Exit 25. Follow signs to Ocean City, which will put you on Route 623 (Roosevelt Boulevard). This road becomes 34th Street in Ocean City. Take this east 1 block and make a left on Simpson. The Historical Museum is in the new, ultramodern Community Center at Simpson and 17th. There's plenty of parking in the Community Center lot.

Ocean City is a big resort with all the modern accouterments: state-of-the-art amusements, a wide boardwalk, oceanfront hotels, and an expansive beach. The town prides itself on its family-oriented image. There is a full calendar of entertainment offerings, including the offbeat and bizarre, like the annual Weird Contest Week in August, which includes things like French fry and salt water taffy sculpting and a wet T-shirt throwing contest, the annual Baby Day Parade, approaching it's ninetieth year, a hot-rodders weekend, the Miss Crustacean Hermit Crab Beauty Pageant and Races, a perennial TV news event, and the Night in Venice Boat Parade, where boat owners dress their crafts like gondolas—or whatever— and cruise the city lagoons. Sound like fun? Hey, fun is Ocean City's middle name.

But unlike many big resort towns that have plowed under their history, Ocean City keeps its history alive.

There is an historic district in town, encompassing most of the blocks from Third Street to Eighth Street (north to south) and from the ocean and Atlantic Avenue five blocks west to

Asbury Avenue. A map of the walking tour is available at the Community Center.

Sites include:

🔖 THE OCEAN CITY TABERNACLE (Fifth Street between Wesley, Central and Asbury), which is the site where Methodist ministers William H. Burrell and the Lake brothers, Wesley, Ezra, and James, founded the Camp Meeting Association on October 20, 1879, establishing Ocean City as a summer resort for Christian families. The first tabernacle was built in 1881, but was taken down by the hurricane of '44. The current brick tabernacle was built in 1957.

🔖 MEMORIAL PARK, across the street from the tabernacle, is where summer worshipers camped in tents (see Ocean Grove, *Monmouth County*). Early costs were a dollar per week for small tents to five and a quarter for the biggest tent. The area today is a war-veterans memorial park.

🔖 THE ORIGINAL TABERNACLE COTTAGES. Twenty-two were built for early worshipers, but only a handful remain including the two at 416 and 418 Ocean Avenue.

🔖 SCOTCH HALL at 435 Wesley Avenue, which was the colonial revival home of Ezra Lake. The home was then converted into a maternity hospital, convalescent home, Coast Guard barracks, and today is a restaurant.

🔖 THE NEW BRIGHTON INN at 519 Fifth Street, which was the Queen Anne Victorian built by William Burrell.

🔖 THE 300 BLOCK OF CENTRAL AVENUE, which has a collection of turn-of-the-century private homes.

🔖 THE 800 BLOCK OF WESLEY AVENUE, which is a neighborhood of large guest-homes.

The condensed version of Ocean City history is, of course, in the historical museum. The museum touches on every aspect and time period of Ocean City life: history, architecture, fashion, commercialism, wildlife, disasters.

A visitor can see things like the bathing suit exhibit from the early 1900s—in twenty years, suits for women went from full and dress-like to skin tight—a photo history of the town's municipal bands and lifesaving crews, pictures of a sixty-two-foot beached whale that washed up in May of 1929, and photos of Chris's Restaurant's Flying Saucer, a hundred-passenger speedboat, from the 1950s.

Some of the most interesting photos are from the disasters: the boardwalk fires of 1921, 1927, and 1928, including a photo of the eerily twisted remains of the carousel; the toppled houses from the storm of '62; an aerial shot of Ocean City submerged during the hurricane of '44.

There are exhibits of carved decoys and stuffed birds, and carved decoys with real feathers glued onto them. The stuffed birds include a great blue heron, a white heron, a hooded merganser, a belted kingfisher, a greater yellowlegs. There are also a stuffed coyote and quail.

There are an original carousel horse from Gillian's Fun Deck and a pair of giant lobster claws brought up from a dredging project that look like something out of B horror movie about mutated sea creatures.

There's a picture of a sixty-eight-foot long finback whale with a thirteen-foot jawbone that washed up in 1891. Thirty-nine people of all sizes climbed onto its back for the photo op.

There are a postcard collection; a Victorian doll collection; Victorian parlors, kitchens, and dining rooms, complete with mannequins in period clothing.

In other words, there's a plate for every palate.

The top attraction at the museum is the *Sindia*. The museum brochure even features an illustration of the four-masted sailing ship. The *Sindia* was a 329-foot, 3,068 ton, four-masted, steel bark built in 1887 in Belfast. Basically, it was a ship caught

between two eras: it was a big, iron-hulled freighter, but powered the old-fashioned way, with winds and canvas.

The *Sindia* was sailing to New York along the Jersey coast, returning from a five-month voyage from Shanghai, via Kobe, Japan. It was loaded with treasures from Asia: hand-painted china and porcelain, elaborate silks and satins, crates of oil of eucalyptus and camphor. During a blizzard on December 15, 1901, the *Sindia* suddenly appeared off the 17th Street beach, headed straight for Ocean City. The crew had mistaken the Cape May Lighthouse for Twin Lights (see Twin Lights, *Monmouth County*) and thought it was pulling into New York Harbor. The ship grounded perpendicular to the beach. The crew tried to swing the ship south, to head for what they hoped was deeper water. That maneuver, coupled with the force of the waves, left the ship parallel to the beach. The Ocean City lifesaving crews launched lifeboats twelve hours later, after the storm subsided, and the thirty-four crewmen were rescued. Efforts to tug the ship off the sand bar failed. Water filled the holds, and a salvage ship came the next day to take whatever it could from the crippled ship. Like a beached whale, the grounded ship drew crowds of thousands, and some of the merchandise from the *Sindia* was sold to onlookers as souvenirs.

The *Sindia* was never towed off the beach. She just sat there and deteriorated, for decades. In time she became as much a part of the Ocean City landscape as any other permanent structure. The wrecked ship was taken for granted, part of the scenery. It belonged to Ocean City.

The museum devotes an entire wing to the *Sindia*. Artifacts include the original figurehead and a replica figurehead carved by Howard Benge. The museum has a sizable collection of *Sindia* cargo: beautiful hand-painted vases and china. The ship's wheel is there, along with numerous photographs and paintings of the wreck. There's even a *Sindia* stained-glass window.

The Cape May County Historical Museum

John Holmes House
504 Route 9
Cape May Courthouse
(609) 465-3535

OPEN: From mid-June to mid-September, Monday through Saturday: 10 A.M. to 4 P.M. From April through mid-June and mid-September through November, Tuesday through Saturday: 10 A.M. to 4 P.M. From December to March, Saturdays: 10 A.M. to 4 P.M.

NOTE: The museum staff conducts tours about every forty minutes, beginning at 10:10 A.M., then 10:50, 11:30, 12:10 P.M., 1:00, 1:40, 2:20, and 3:00, which is the last tour of day.

COST: $2 for adults, 50-cents for children under 12, children under 2 are free.

DIRECTIONS: Exit 10 or 13 on the Garden State Parkway will take you to Cape May Courthouse on Route 9. The museum is about 1 mile south of the downtown area.

🐦 The Dutch hunted whales off Cape May in the 1630s. The English came down from New England a few years later and expanded the practice. From about 1640 to 1700, the Cape May area was a whaling center, with entire villages devoted to either the hunt and kill or the dissection of the carcass. The whalers were so successful that they eventually killed their own industry. As whales around the Cape grew scarce, many of the original New England whaling families went into another line of work, or moved further up the Jersey Coast or back to New England.

Whaling's importance in the colonization of the Cape cannot be underestimated. Thirty-five prominent families, whose early livelihood was tied to whaling, became the anchor of Cape May County government and industry of all kinds. By the 1690s their farms and estates, ranging from fifty to six hundred and fifty acres, ran in a loosely connected line from Great Egg Harbor down to the tip of Cape May. Yet there is very little preserved from the whaling days. In fact, the Cape May Historical Museum is one of the few places where whaling instruments, harpoons and harpoon guns, and whale bones are on display. Whale teeth were popular for carvers and other folk artists, and the museum has a collection of whale tooth art (scrimshaw).

These artifacts can be seen in the barn portion of the John Holmes House. There are other maritime items on display, too, like sextants and telescopes, early shipbuilding tools, ship models, the spy glass belonging to Israel Leaming, and the original ten-foot tall lens from the Cape May Lighthouse.

The barn has some other interesting things: a rattlesnake killed in Cape May Court House in 1914, a bald eagle shot in Dias Creek in 1905, Indian artifacts, a ribbon from the *Lusitania,* a decoy duck collection, a cedar shingle mining exhibit, a stage coach, a peddler's wagon, and a doctor's sulky.

There are some interesting things in the main house, especially in the museum's military room. Here one will find a flag from the U.S.S. *Merrimac,* the iron-sided gunboat of Civil War fame, and drum ropes from the War of 1812.

Dennisville-Goshen Area

DIRECTIONS: Route 47 in Cape May County goes through the heart of Goshen and Dennisville. The Dennisville Historic District is slightly northeast of the highway, situated on the blocks of Academy, Church, Fidler, Hall, Main, and Petersburg roads and part of Route 47.

Shipbuilding and cedar-shingle "mining" were the principal industries in the Dennisville-Goshen area. The boat yards at Dennisville and Goshen can be traced back to the 1700s, but were at their busiest from 1859 to 1898. In 1883 alone, eleven ships were constructed in Dennisville, launched sideways into the narrow Dennis Creek, and sailed out into the Delaware Bay.

There were three major shipyards in the Goshen-Dennisville area: Garrison and Harker on Goshen Creek, Richard S. Leaming at Dennis Creek and Jesse H. Diverty also at Dennis Creek.

Many of the ships made in these yards were substantial. Leaming produced an eight hundred-ton ocean schooner called the *William E. Lee* in 1877, but most were in the two hundred- to three hundred-ton neighborhood.

In late 1800s two things happened to cripple the shipbuilding industry: railroads became more prevalent, thereby eliminating the need for coastal schooners; and the Dennis and Goshen creeks began to fill in, making it more difficult for shipbuilders to launch substantial boats and get them out to the bay.

The men in the area not employed in shipbuilding during the 1800s were either farmers or lumber "miners." The swamp around Dennisville is home to a prehistoric forest, broken down and preserved in the airless muck. Miners found the logs by using a metal rod about eight-feet long to poke through the marshy wetlands until they hit something solid. Then, using a long saw, they would cut out a piece of test wood, to see if the buried lumber was worth salvaging. The degree of rot would determine a log's worth. The less rot, the better the wood. Once the logs were unearthed and brought to the surface, they were cut into shingles. Sounds like hard, dirty work? Well it was. But it was profitable, and there was high demand for Dennisville roof shingles. Lumber mines were established in the area, yielding about a half-million shingles and two hundred thousand cedar rails a year in their heyday. The shingles had a reputation of being top-notch; they were estimated to last a hundred years. Some twenty-five thousand of the shingles were used to reroof Independence Hall in Philadelphia in the 1860s.

The industry was done in by the invention of asphalt roofing materials. For those who insisted on wooden shingles, modern lumber yards could produce good quality shingles much cheaper than the Dennisville shingle miners. So the business died, but long before miners exhausted the supply of trees in the sunken forest. They are still there, tapped occasionally by wood crafts-man and artists who need high quality wood.

Despite the economic downturns of a century ago, Dennisville and Goshen have kept up their appearances. Dennisville's sixty-nine-building, eight-block historic district rivals Greenwich and Mauricetown (see *Cumberland County*) for mint condition historic homes. These homes were built by sea captains, shipyard owners, merchants, and the main founders of the town, such as Nathaniel Holmes, whose home still stands on Main Street.

The Dennisville Historic District is listed on both state and national historic registers. Historic-house tours are given twice a year, organized by the Dennisville Historic Home Owner's Association.

Goshen's historic district is not as substantial, but there are some interesting buildings, such as the Goshen Methodist Church and the public school, with it's gabled front and center bell tower. Most of Goshen's historic structures are right along Route 47.

Hereford Inlet Lighthouse

First and Central Avenues
North Wildwood
(609) 522-4520 or (609) 522-2030

OPEN: Mid-May to the end of September, daily: 9 A.M. to 5 P.M. Off-season, Mondays and Thursday through Sunday: 11 A.M. to 3 P.M.

COST: Donations accepted.

DIRECTIONS: Take the Garden State Parkway to Exit 6, and Route 147 east into North Wildwood, which becomes Jersey Avenue. Make a left on First Street. The lighthouse is 1 block down on First and Central.

When people think of lighthouses, they usually visualize the vertigo-inspiring towers of Sandy Hook, Barnegat, or Cape May with their long spiral staircases to the top.

The big tower lighthouses along the Jersey Coast are the most famous: everyone knows Sandy Hook is the oldest working lighthouse in the nation; Old Barney attracts thousands of visitors a year to the northern tip of Long Beach Island, and the Cape May climb rewards the hardy tourist with a bird's eye view of some of the best bird-watching territory in the world.

The giant beacons were not the most common lighthouses along the Jersey Coast. The shoreline—the Atlantic and Delaware Bay sides—was dotted with smaller structures that were lighthouses in the most literal sense. These beacons, which marked inlets and coves, were usually three-story homes with a cupola, or tower, that housed a beacon. The lightkeeper and his family lived in the rest of the house.

On the Delaware side only the East Point Lighthouse remains (see *Cumberland County*). Small, residential lighthouses at Egg Island and the Maurice and Cohansey rivers were sold at public auctions, then abandoned, and eventually torn down.

On the Atlantic side, there were residential lighthouses at Point Comfort in Keansburg, Chapel Hill near Leonardo; Sea Girt; the Ludlum Light in Sea Isle City, the Hereford Inlet Lighthouse in Angelsea, or North Wildwood; and Tucker's Island.

Of those, two were done in by the elements: Tucker's Island and the Ludlum Light. Two were converted into privates homes: Chapel Hill, which still stands, and Point Comfort, which was destroyed by fire. Two were converted to public use: Sea Girt is owned by the town and used for town functions, and Hereford is open to the public.

Hereford is the only lighthouse of its kind on the East Coast,

The Hereford Lighthouse.

though it has a twin in California, between the San Francisco and San Pablo bays.

For lack of a better term, Hereford is known as a Victorian lighthouse, and its surroundings, these days, certainly create the image of a gentler time. The grounds are like a park. Brick and grass paths, benches, and a gazebo are surrounded by shrubs, flower gardens, wild flowers, and herb gardens. The lighthouse grounds are so beautiful, it is becoming an increasingly popular place for weddings. There are crafts shows and concerts. The inside is laid out like a gallery. Fine art will be hung and nautical museum is planned.

This air of elegance belies Hereford's violent and tragic past.

Like any lighthouse, it was born of necessity. Ships were crashing and men were drowning at the inlet. The fishermen from Angelsea, as North Wildwood was known, organized a life-saving service in 1849. By 1871 Congress realized the inlet needed a permanent facility. As commercial activity in the inlet increased, so did ship groundings and wrecks. The Life Saving Station was given a light, which became operational on May 11, 1874.

The first lightkeeper, John Nick, drowned. Then the lighthouse was under constant attack by the sea. The beach in front of it was eroded away, and, finally, a storm in 1913 threatened the structure. The waves washed away the high sand dune on which the lighthouse was built, exposing one side of the foundation to the surf.

The lighthouse had to be either abandoned, torn down, or moved. Engineers came up with a plan, and the lighthouse was safely moved about a hundred and fifty feet inland. Today, it is about two hundred and fifty feet from the water line. The almighty sea continues to giveth and taketh away.

Visitors to Hereford can stroll the grounds and climb the tower. The lighthouse is currently home to the North Wildwood Tourist Information Center, and there are a number of exhibits on North Wildwood history.

The George F. Boyer Historical Museum
(The **Wildwood Historical Museum** and **National Marbles Hall of Fame**)

3907 Pacific Avenue
Holly Beach Mall
Wildwood
(609) 523-0277

OPEN: Summers, Monday through Friday: 9:30 A.M. to 2:30 P.M.; Friday evenings: 6:30 P.M. to 8:30 P.M.; and Saturdays and Sundays: 10:30 A.M. to 2:30 P.M. October 1 to May 1, Thursday through Sunday: 10:30 A.M. to 2:30 P.M.

COST: Donations accepted.

DIRECTIONS: Take the Garden State Parkway to Exit 4 and follow Route 47 east into Wildwood. Make a right on New Jersey Avenue and head north. Go about 6 blocks and look for Spencer. Make a left on Spencer and go 1 block to the Holly Beach Mall (an outdoor "Main Street" closed to vehicular traffic). The museum is near the Spencer Avenue entrance to the mall.

NOTE: If you're coming to the Wildwood Museum from the Hereford Lighthouse, simply go back to New Jersey Avenue and go south about 1 mile to Spencer.

Okay, so it's not Cooperstown, but to the kids who play marbles on the Wildwood beach for the national championship each year, the stakes are as high as any World Series. The shrine to the winners . . . the champions . . . the immortals of marbles . . . is part of the Boyers Museum. In terms of national competitions designed to bring tourists to the shore, the marbles contest is pre-dated only by the Miss America Pageant. In 1922 Bud McQuade won the first marbles championship. The tournament has been played every year since, except for 1944 and 1945, because of World War II.

Like baseball, or any other sport, marbles reflects the changing American landscape. Many cultural historians trace the beginnings of the modern women's movement to World War II, when

*Ready . . . aim. . . . The national marbles competition at Wildwood (1950s)
required a steady hand and nerves of steel. Courtesy of
George F. Boyer Historical Museum.*

housewives and young women went to work to support the war
effort, never again content to stay home. Marbles was on the cutting edge: the first girls' championship was instituted in 1948.

The misty-eyed sports romantics who think that only baseball is a microcosm of changing America should take a look at
marbles. In 1986 Giang Duong, a boy of Vietnamese heritage,
won the championship. His brother, Bong Duong, won in 1994.
The Babe Ruth of marbles is, without question, Debra Stanley
of Pennsylvania. She won the tournament in 1973, then coached
seven winners—both boys and girls—and was the assistant
coach for two others. Two of Stanley's protégés were the Stamm
sisters, Patricia and Nicole, each girls' winners in the early '80s.
Their brother, Danny Stamm, won the boys' title in 1979, giving credence to the theory that the steady hand and steely eye
needed to win at marbles are more determined by genes than
environment.

Wildwood hosts the marbles championship every June, drawing about a hundred girls and boys from around the nation. The contestants square off in ten concrete marbles courts on the beach—many pictures show the kids wearing knee pads . . . you've gotta protect the knees for the long haul—competing for $2,000 in scholarships and prizes, and immortality in the National Marbles Hall of Fame.

The rest of the Boyers Museum lives up to its motto: "Come see the Wildwood that Grandpa knew." If grandpa were around today, he could see photographs of the lone fishing shacks on the island from the 1870s and 1880s, the first wood bridge that connected Wildwood with the mainland in 1884, and the first railroad stop, also built in 1884, which brought passengers from near Cape May Court House to Angelsea. With a railroad in place, Wildwood became a vacationland. Hotels went up. Amusement piers went up. Crowds came. And they're still coming today.

The first marbles competition was in 1922, making the national competition the longest running event at the Shore after the Miss America Pageant. Courtesy of George F. Boyer Historical Museum.

The museum's photograph and postcard collection will help grandpa remember all the landmarks . . . everything from the old Marine Pier amusement area on the boardwalk to the Sheldon Hotel on Magnolia and Atlantic to Ed Zaberers restaurant.

Zaberers burned down in 1992, and the Firemen's and Policemen's Room in the museum has a wall filled with pictures of some of the town's most spectacular and disastrous fires: the Ocean Pier blaze in 1943, the Starlight Ballroom in 1981, and the Nickels Midway Pier in 1992.

Those places are gone, but their memory lives on in the minds of thousands of grandpas who knew Wildwood, and at the Boyers Museum.

Cape May (City)

> DIRECTIONS: Take the Garden State Parkway south until the end. Continue straight into Cape May.

Widely acknowledged as the nation's most enduring seaside resort, Cape May today is a national treasure . . . not just because of its past, but because so much of the past is visible today.

Cape May is a charmer, all right. The entire town has National Historic Landmark status, and the brightly colored Victorian homes, guest houses, and hotels make it one of the best walking-around towns anywhere. The town has a number of first-class restaurants and elegant bed-and-breakfast inns. The beachfront is lined with grande dame hotels of every size, mixed in with some young giants.

In summer Cape May seems less crowded than other popular resorts. The boardwalk has a lot of activity, but the absence of amusement piers gives everyone more elbow room. The boardwalk on the east end of town has no commercial businesses or arcades . . . just moonlight on the water and the sound of lapping waves.

Historically, Cape May City was a bit behind some other parts of the county in growth. The whalers down from New England, many of whom were descendants of Mayflower families, set up on the bay side of the cape and called their little colony Town Bank, not to be confused with today's Town Bank. The original Town Bank was on land that is now under water. Farming further north in the cape (around Cape May Court House) proved to be a more reliable and less dangerous way to make a living than fishing. The point of the cape was raw and rough, and the convergence of the bay and ocean made for unpredictable seas and dramatic erosion. Stephen Decatur, one of the many famous visitors to Cape May, surveyed the point and concluded that the point was actually three miles longer in ancient times. In modern times, two lighthouses at the point were lost to the sea before the existing lighthouse was built in 1859 (see Cape May Lighthouse).

The second lighthouse, which came down in 1847, figured prominently in a Philadelphia newspaper ad on June 30, 1801, which, by all accounts, is Cape May's first entry into the tourist trade. The ad, placed by Ellis Hughes, who was trying to lure guests to his new Hotel Atlantic, described Cape May this way: "The situation is beautiful, just at the confluence of Delaware Bay and ocean, in sight of the Lighthouse and affords a view of shipping which enters and leaves the Delaware . . . It is the most delightful spot citizens can retire to in the hot season."

Within a few years, Cape May became a popular summer spot for wealthy Philadelphians, who came in coastal sloops and schooners. Competition sprang up around Hughes. Hotel were going up, attracting more visitors. Ellis's son, Thomas, built the first Congress Hall in 1815. In 1819 steamboats were ferrying people down the Delaware from Philadelphia. Cape May became very popular among Washingtonians, Virginians, and other Southern gentry. Perhaps that's why builder Philip Cain chose the name Mount Vernon for a massive 482-room hotel he built in Cape May in 1853; Cain died in a fire that destroyed the hotel in 1856. Presidents Franklin Pierce and James Buchanan came in the 1850s; Lincoln came as early as 1849.

Of course, many of the gentry left their good-breeding and manners at home when they came to Cape May. According to author Jeffery M. Dorwart in his book *Cape May County, New Jersey* (Rutgers University Press) the council "passed ordinances to 'suppress riotous conduct,' prohibit the explosion of fireworks and prevent swimming without 'suitable bathing apparel.'" Dorwart also documents a riot between some of the Southern "gentlemen" and the free black hotel workers which one witness says, "caused some bloody heads." Dorwart writes of "the Blue Pig, a notorious Cape Island gambling den" and of the "hundreds of young men and women (who) ate, drank, danced the 'hop,' set off firecrackers, and romped until the early hours of the morning."

Nowadays, if you want that kind of action, you're better off in Seaside, where one four-cornered intersection has seven bars.

The crackdown changed Cape May into a more conservative resort. The young Southerners stop coming during the Civil War and the town became decidedly more placid in summer months.

The big build-up in Cape May came after the war, especially in the 1870s and 1880s, although the town suffered an economic slump during some of that time. Many of the most picturesque homes are from that era, including the Emlen Physick Estate (1879) at 1048 Washington Street. The Physick Estate is Victorian through and through and open for tours (call 609 884-5404). There is also a tour and afternoon tea at The Abbey (1869) on Gurney and Columbia (609 884-4506). Both homes are virtual Victorian museums. Great for fans of architecture and fancy furnishings, but brutal for children. You and other tour-goers will have a better time if you leave the children at home.

Other sites in and around Cape May:

The Cape May Visitors' Center

405 Lafayette St. (at Decatur)
(609) 884-9562

OPEN: Daily: 9 A.M. to 4:30 P.M.

This the best place to start if you want to tour Cape May. The center has all the brochures and supplies copies of *This Week in Cape May*, the most comprehensive guide to activities you'll find. Every resort town should consider doing this. The visitors' center is in a pre-Civil War Presbyterian Church, a perfect warm-up for the other historic buildings you'll see.

The Church of Our Lady "Star of the Sea" Catholic Church

On the Mall at intersection of Washington Street and Ocean Avenue
(609) 884-5312

OPEN: Church is open to visitors almost all the time, but those not wishing to attend Mass should not enter the church when Mass is being celebrated.

The church, built in 1911, isn't in the Victorian mode, but it is one the most beautiful stops in town. The stained-glass windows alone are worth the visit. The back window, of Mary ascending into heaven, faces south and gets good background light all day. On a typical Cape May summer day, the Mary window glows like subdued neon. The maritime theme is present in many of the windows, especially the large window to the right of the altar, which features an ocean scene with wooden sailing ships. A slow walk through the church is a peaceful and cool respite from outdoor sightseeing or shopping.

The Greater Cape May Historical Society (The Colonial House)

> 653 Washington Street
> No phone

OPEN: Mid-June to mid-September, daily: 1 P.M. to 4 P.M. Closed the rest of the year.

The Colonial House, Cape May's oldest home (1775), is truly a hidden treasure. It sits in the back of a deep lot on Washington Street next to City Hall, but is partially hidden by Alexander's Restaurant. It is one of the few places in town where Victorian does not rule. The rooms are filled with artifacts from the 1700s, and the museum offers exhibits that don't always focus on the town's Victorian past. In the summer of 1995, they had an exhibit on the great storms of Cape May. The year before, it was a railroad display. The 1996 exhibit features the Christian Admiral Hotel.

The Cape May Firemen's Museum

> Corner of Washington and Franklin Streets
> No phone

OPEN: Daily: 9 A.M. to 5 P.M.

When a Cape May fireman strolls down one of his town's shady streets and sees the Victorian homes standing shoulder to shoulder, he can see the ornate gingerbread woodwork, the handcut wood shingles and the decorative pastel-colored trim work. He can see the old giant, rambling wooden hotels like the Chalfonte. But he also sees something the average walk-about tourist doesn't see: the potential for disaster.

Fires, more than nature's violent storms, have been the town's disaster legacy.

The Mount Vernon Hotel, billed as the world's largest hotel when construction began in 1853, went down in 1856. As land values doubled in Cape May after the Civil War, property owners turned to arson to clear their land of ramshackle buildings. A fire in 1869 wiped out the old section along Jackson and Ocean Streets.

The rash of fires called for the formation of a fire department, and the Cape May company was chartered in 1875.

Three years later, they found themselves fighting the grandpappy of all fires. On November 9, 1878, a fire started in the Ocean House and took down forty acres of hotels, cottages, and beachfront bath houses between Congress and Gurney Streets. The fire was so bad, firefighting equipment and volunteers came in by rail from Camden and Millville, although they arrived too late to save many of the buildings. The property casualties were the biggest names in Cape May: The Atlantic Hotel, Congress Hall, Columbia House, Centre House, and the Ocean House. The fire legacy lives on: wood craftsman Franz Biehl, who did the woodworking restoration on the classic George Allen House on Washington Street in 1994–1995, milled poplar, white oak, red oak, cherry burl and maple trees from the property for the project. He said a number of the trees showed signs of scorching from the fire, which came up to Allen's property but did not damage the house.

Big fires continued through the rest of the ninth and twentieth centuries. In 1903 the Marine Villa Hotel, one of the town's giants, went down. The Cape May Mall was consumed in 1976. The Windsor Hotel burned down in 1979. The Chalfonte survived, but took a big hit in 1975. A year later it was the Baronet's turn.

Every generation of Cape May firemen has fought at least one historical blaze. Like a proud war veteran's group, they decided to build a museum to preserve their legacy. The firemen's museum has pictures of most of the town's big blazes and roster photographs of many of the companies that fought them. There are displays of antique equipment, including a 1928 LaFrance pumper truck.

JOHN DI IONNO

The Cape May Firemen's Museum.

The only thing not antique is the museum building, which many people think is the original Cape May firehouse. The museum building is a replica of the original, built on approximately the same spot. The new firehouse, with bays for six big trucks and ambulances, is behind it.

Today's Cape May Fire Department is made up of ten full-timers, who are also certified Emergency Medical Technicians, and thirty-five volunteers; they're always looking for more.

"We're all locals and it's getting harder to get young guys to volunteer," said paid fireman Robert Elwell, Jr., a young guy himself and a fourth-generation Cape May fireman." And we need all the guys we can get. You never know when you're going to need them."

The Fishermen's Memorial

End of Missouri Avenue
Cape May

OPEN: Dawn to dusk.

COST: Free.

DIRECTIONS: Take the Garden State Parkway to its end and continue into Cape May. Make a left on Sidney and a right on Washington. Go 2 blocks and make a left on West Avenue. West will take you to Missouri Avenue. Continue straight to the end.

"He hushed the storm to a gentle breeze and the billows of the sea were stilled . . ."
—BIBLICAL INSCRIPTION ON THE FISHERMEN'S MEMORIAL

On a dead-end street in Cape May—far from the gingerbread guest houses, the oceanfront hotels, the five-star restaurants, the beaches and boardwalk—a lonely woman stands, clutching her two children as she looks out over the harbor. She is waiting for her fisherman husband to return from the sea. She will wait forever. The fatherless family is carved in granite and stands as the memorial to all lost fisherman in the Cape May area.

"That's the perpetuity and reality of it," said Beech Fox, the man who got the idea for the monument, which was erected in 1988. "Fisherman will continue to go to sea and continue to lose their lives."

The monument lists the names of all the Cape May–area fishermen who have been lost at sea since the mid-1800s. Some of the family names are hauntingly repeated from generation to generation to generation. Fishing being a family business, there are also many incidents where more than one family member, father and sons, brother and brother, went down on the same ship.

And the list goes on. The dangers of making a daily living on the ocean have subsided a bit since a century ago. Electronic distress signals, radar, speedy search-and-rescue Coast Guard operations by air and sea, better weather-predicting technology, and stronger, more sea-worthy boats have significantly slowed the loss of life at sea. But there are still tragedies, times "when the waves turn the minutes to hours."

Every few years, the stone carvers go out and add a few names to the tablet on the memorial.

"We have a half-dozen or so names to add right now, right up until the men who were lost last year," Fox said.

U.S. Coast Guard Station

Cape May
(609) 898-6969 (for tour information)

OPEN: The base is open to the public for self-guided tours Monday through Saturday: 9 A.M. to 11 A.M. and 1 P.M. to 3 P.M.

COST: Free.

DIRECTIONS: Take the Garden State Parkway to its end and continue into Cape May. Make a left on Sidney Avenue, a left on Washington, a quick right on Texas. Go 2 blocks and make a right on Pittsburgh. Go 5 blocks and make a left on Pennsylvania, which runs into the main entrance of the Coast Guard Station. If this sounds confusing, don't worry. The path to the base is well-marked.

The four hundred and fifty-acre Coast Guard Station lies between the Atlantic Ocean and the Cape May harbor. Visitors to the base get a tour brochure and map and are free to go into designated areas. Since the base is the nation's only Coast Guard recruit training center, or boot camp, there is a good chance you'll see cadets on the drill field during summer months.

The Cape May Coast Guard Station is the biggest in New Jersey and covers a wide range of the Atlantic and all of the Delaware Bay for search-and-rescue and law enforcement, often working in concert with the station at Sandy Hook.

Down at the docks, the Coast Guard keeps a small fleet, including a 210-foot medium endurance cutter, a 180-foot buoy tender, a 110-foot law-enforcement vessel, two 80-foot patrol boats, and four other boats under 50 feet.

The Coast Guard also has three helicopters at the base that go out on routine patrol. It is not unusual to see the red choppers buzzing up and down the Cape May beachfront.

The base has a number of monuments, but the biggest pays tribute to Douglas Monroe, the Coast Guard's only Medal of Honor recipient. Monroe was killed while trying to rescue Marines at Guadalcanal.

JOHN DI IONNO

The Coast Guard Station in Cape May.

In addition to the self-guided tours, the public is also invited to weekly Friday afternoon graduation ceremonies of Coast Guard recruits, which includes a pass-and-review parade in warm weather months. There are also a number of public sunset parades during the summer, which include a pass-and-review parade and the lowering of the colors. These are usually held on major holidays and around August 4, the Coast Guard's official birthday. Call (609) 898-6969.

The Cape May Lighthouse and Cape May Point State Park

> End of Lighthouse Road
> Cape May Point
> (609) 884-2159
> For lighthouse information call (609) 884-5404

OPEN: The park, daily: DAWN to DUSK. The park museum, Memorial Day to Labor Day: 8 A.M. to 8 P.M. Off-season, every day but Mondays and Tuesdays: 8 A.M. to 3:15 P.M.

LIGHTHOUSE HOURS AND INFORMATION: call (609) 884-5404. The lighthouse is run by the Mid-Atlantic Center for the Arts, and hours are determined by the availability of volunteer members. Generally, the lighthouse is open every day in summer, and on weekend afternoons only in winter.

COST: The park, which has a beach, bird-watching areas and nature trails, is free, as is the museum. Lighthouse fees are $3 for adults; New Jersey children are free. Out-of-state students are $1.

DIRECTIONS: Take the Garden State Parkway to its end and continue into Cape May. You will be on Lafayette Street. At end of Lafayette, near the town bandstand and visitors' center, make a right on Jackson. Jackson goes into West Perry, which becomes Sunset. Follow this 2 miles and make a left on Lighthouse Road. The lighthouse towers over the area, so it's easy to spot, and there are a number of signs leading to it.

The Cape May Point State Park has sunbathing, surf fishing, and bird watching—three of the staples of shore outdoor recreation—all accessible from the same parking lot. And, believe it or not, it's the bird watching that draws the biggest crowd. The annual hawk count, taken during September and October, fills the parking lot with so many cars, you'd think it was Fourth of July weekend. The state park is just one in a series of wildlife refuges and areas that make the cape the capital of East Coast bird watching and an internationally-known hot spot. (The Cape May Bird Observatory's Northwood Center is right around the corner on East Lake Drive, off

JOHN DI IONNO

The Cape May Hawkwatch, 1994.

Lighthouse Road.) Not only is the cape rich in indigenous birds, but is an important way station for hundred of species that migrate south in the fall, and back north in the spring.

The museum gives an explanation of the migratory routes of birds and maps of flight patterns. There is also an exhibit on sea life, including whale bones, a loggerhead turtle skull and other turtle shells, and a horseshoe crab exhibit.

The lighthouse offers 199 steps to the top and long lines to get in, during summer, but the panoramic view of Cape May City and the Atlantic and Delaware Bay shorelines is worth it.

The lighthouse, built in 1859, is the third on the tip of the cape. The earliest known beacon used there was a "flash light" in 1744, used to guide whalers and other sailing ships around the cape and into the bay. The first lighthouse was built in 1823, and washed away into the sea. Another one went up in 1847, but erosion jeopardized it even before it became operational. The current lighthouse was built one-third of a mile back, and should be on safe ground for the next couple of centuries.

In 1994 the lighthouse underwent a major restoration. Today it is run by the Mid-Atlantic Center for the Arts, which

JOHN DI IONNO

Birding is big business at Cape May point.

Cape May Lighthouse recently underwent a major renovation.

leases it from the state. The former oil house at the base of the tower serves as a gift shop and museum.

The Concrete Ship

> End of Sunset Boulevard
> Cape May Point

> DIRECTIONS: Take the Garden State Parkway to its end and continue into Cape May, you will be on Lafayette Street. At end of Lafayette, near the town bandstand and visitors' center, make a right on Jackson. Jackson goes into West Perry, which becomes Sunset. Follow to its end.

 Like the lost continent of Atlantis, the U.S.S. *Atlantus* is sinking into the sea.

The broken hull of the *Atlantus,* more widely-known as the concrete ship, is a hundred yards off of Sunset Beach, stuck in the sand, right where it's been for most of this century. Seventy years of storms, strong currents, and the relentless washing of waves and tides have the ship disintegrating, disappearing right before our eyes.

The ship, a monument to a bad idea gone worse, was a novelty long before it sank into the sand at Sunset Beach. Toward the end of World War I, when steel was in short supply, the U.S. Navy commissioned the construction of forty-three concrete ships. Only twelve were built, including the *Atlantus,* which slipped out of drydock into the water a month after the war ended. The *Atlantus* made a couple of troop runs, bringing home America's victorious and war-weary soldiers, before being sent to a naval graveyard in Norfolk, Virginia, called Pig Point. The *Atlantus* stayed there from 1921 until 1926, while salvagers picked it clean of anything of value.

Plans for a Cape May to Lewes, Delaware, ferry were taking shape and the ship was purchased by the National Navigation Company, head by Col. Jesse Rosenfeld. According to most historical accounts, the *Atlantus* and three other concrete ships were to be sunk in a Y pattern to form the base of the ferry dock at Cape May Point. The *Atlantus* was towed to Cape May in June of 1926 and moored offshore. The ship broke away from it's mooring during the next storm and came to rest in the sand off the beach. Attempts to refloat it failed, and towing the two hundred and fifty-foot freighter proved futile. So it stayed. And sank deeper and deeper into the sand.

A plaque in the beach parking lot explains the story of the ship and, after nature runs its course, that's all there will be.

No discussion of the concrete ship would be complete, however, without mentioning the two other attractions at Sunset Beach: Cape May diamonds and the flag-lowering ceremony.

The diamonds are pure quartz crystals from interior rock formations far up the Delaware. The crystals are brought down the river and into the bay by the swift current. And then, according to Sunset Beach proprietor Marvin Hume, they are polished by the turbulent waters—and the concrete ship.

"The swift tide of the Delaware brings them down, and the swirls around our concrete ship eddies the mix," Hume said. "If it wasn't for that concrete ship, there wouldn't be any Cape

JOHN DI OONNO

The Concrete Ship at Sunset Beach is slowly disappearing into the sea.

May diamonds. But because of that ship, every outgoing tide brings us a fresh batch of diamonds."

Almost as dependable as the tide is Hume's flag-lowering ceremony. Each evening at sunset the American flag is lowered at Sunset Beach in a solemn ceremony that attracts about a hundred people a night.

"We have people come from all over the country to see our ceremony," Hume said.

For more than two decades, Marvin Hume has presided over the flag-lowering ceremony on the beach as the sun sinks into the expansive Delaware Bay. Sunset Beach, the western tip of the cape, and the belly of Cumberland County are the only places in New Jersey—and among only a handful on the entire East Coast—where you can see the sun set over water.

"The previous owner started the ceremony and did it for about fifteen years. I took over (in 1974), and we've been doing it ever since."

The ceremony is held every evening from Memorial Day to Labor Day, and on weekend nights from May 1 to Memorial Day and from Labor Day to the end of October.

"It's a time to honor the flag and the country," said Hume, a World War II navy veteran. "We ask people to stand quietly and honor the flag during the ceremony. If they're sitting in their cars, we ask them to get out and stand and join us."

The ceremony begins with a recording of Kate Smith's "God Bless America," followed by a U.S. Army Band's rendition of "The Star-Spangled Banner." The flag comes down to the lonely sound of a single bugler blowing "Taps."

"The flags we use are casket flags donated to us by the families of deceased veterans," Hume said, adding that there's never a shortage of flags, despite the high winds at Sunset Beach that tatter between six and eight flags a season. "I put one ad in the paper (when he started) requesting a casket flag and I've never had to do it again. They just keep coming in. It's a family's way of honoring its veteran."

Cumberland County

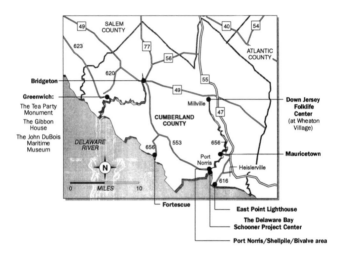

Want to get away from it all? A trip to Cumberland County will do the trick. You can drive miles through farmlands and pastures, through swamps and grassy marshes, without ever encountering another vehicle—in either direction. Cumberland is New Jersey's wide open spaces—a vast county anchored by two big towns, Millville and Bridgeton, and dotted by a number of sleepy villages. Despite a well-organized tourism board and an active historical society, Cumberland County remains a well-kept secret to most Jerseyans. The county's distance from North Jersey—it's about three and a half hours from the Newark area—makes it a long day for a day trip, and lodging is scarce. Picturesque Mauricetown, for instance, does not even have a restaurant, let along a bed-and-breakfast. Travelers will do best to reserve a weekend for exploring Cumberland, and to find a place to stay in the major centers.

Town of Greenwich

DIRECTIONS: Greenwich is most easily reached one of
three ways off Route 49. FROM SALEM, follow signs to
Greenwich, which takes you to Route 623 south, which
is called New Bridge Road, the Harmersville-Canton
Road, and the Greenwich Cumberland Causeway Road,
all within the 10 miles it takes to get to Greenwich Center. FROM SHILOH, farther east off Route 49, find Route
620 south (called the Greenwich-Shiloh Road) and take
it to Route 623 and continue south. This is about a 6
mile trip. FROM BRIDGETON, take Route 650 (Dutch
Neck Road) south, then west as it becomes Sheppard's
Mill Road. Take Route 650 to Route 607 south, which
is called Bridge-on-Greenwich Road, which is leads into
the heart of Greenwich, Ye Greate Street.

Here's the most important thing to remember when
visiting Greenwich: mosquito repellent. The little bloodsuck-
ers can ruin what otherwise is one of the most delightful trips
you can make along the Jersey coast. In Greenwich the mosquito quickly outgrows nuisance status. In just a few arm-slap-
ping moments, they become elevated to most hated enemy, one
which needs to be stamped out regardless of the chemical con-
sequences. Legend has it that the Delaware Bay mosquito forced
Swedish settlers to abandon Fort Elfsborg, just miles upriver
in Salem County, and the swampy marshlands along the Delaware and Cohansey rivers in Greenwich are equally infested.

Mosquitoes aside, Greenwich is one of New Jersey's "great
quaints"—small towns off the beaten path that remain largely
unchanged over the centuries.

History is so important to the village, the main street's name
was changed back a few years ago to it's original form—Ye
Greate Street.

Greenwich may be one of the first truly "diverse" towns in
America. Founded in 1675 as a sister settlement to Salem (see
Salem County) by John Fenwick's son-in-law Samuel Hedge,

William Penn, surveyor Richard Tindall, and Samuel Smith of Smithfield, it was determined to be a place full of religious tolerance. Before his death, Fenwick had laid out the community in sixteen-acre lots, and the first lot owner was Mark Reeve, an English Quaker. In short order came Baptist Thomas Watson and Nicholas Gibbon, an Episcopalian, who gave some of his land to a group of Presbyterians.

Before the turn of the century, foreign ships were using Greenwich as a port of entry for towns upriver, such as Philadelphia and Burlington. By the 1730s, six taverns sprung up in town to accommodate visiting merchants and ship crews. Sea captains settled there. The stage stopped there. It was a bustling port town and, in its early days, bigger than Philadelphia. It's amazing that such an optimistic, flowing start could turn into such a slow trickle of economic progress. Who knows why history turns its course elsewhere, putting one town in the mainstream of growth, and leaving another behind? In the case of Greenwich, maybe it was the mosquitoes.

Of course, Greenwich didn't go quietly. A tea burning incident there in 1774 reverberated through the colonies. In 1908 a ceremony to unveil a monument to the tea-burners drew eight thousand people from all over South Jersey.

The little town is proud of it's history, and there has been a resurgence of historical pride in the village for the last thirty years, due mostly to Mrs. Sarah Watson, the president of the historical society.

"Without Mrs. Watson, there wouldn't be this interest," said Ruth Jackson, a historical society member. "She has devoted her life to this town and to the history of the county as a whole."

With pride in history comes diligent preservation. There seems to be an unspoken rule in Greenwich that little should be changed. A walking-tour map of the Greenwich historic district shows fifty-seven historic homes dating from the early

1700s to the 1930s. The post-1930 buildings include two residences and a bank.

Here is our own walk down Ye Greate Street in Greenwich.

The Tea Party Monument

> Corner of Ye Greate Street and Market Lane
> Greenwich

The monument basically looks like the only gravemarker in a small cemetery, surrounded by a black, wrought-iron fence. It sits alone in a corner lot, an eight-foot high stone structure with a large bronze plaque depicting men disguised as Indians burning tea in a bonfire. The names of many of the tea-burners are engraved in the monument.

The incident occurred on December 22, 1774, a year after the more famous Boston Tea Party. The British brig *Greyhound* was destined for Philadelphia, but its captain had heard that American patriots might make a symbolic torch out of his shipment of heavily taxed British tea. In fact, a ship loaded with tea had been turned away from the Philadelphia docks just weeks earlier. The *Greyhound*'s captain decided to duck up the Cohansey River and unload his tea shipment at the home of British sympathizer Daniel Bowen. Bowen allowed the tea to be stored in his basement and word spread among the Cumberland County patriots. According to author William McMahon in *South Jersey Towns—History and Legends* (Rutgers University Press) a committee was formed to deal with the matter. McMahon writes, "This committee, comprised of thirty-five citizens of the area, decided to proceed with caution. The more militant and youthful element decided to take matters into their own hands."

This young and "militant" group decided to dress as Indians, complete with war-painted faces, and have their own "tea party." The group numbered twenty-three, including eight sets of brothers: the Elmers, Ewings, Fithians, Howells, Hunts,

Newcombs, Piersons, and Seeleys, all names immortalized on the monument. They broke into Bowen's home and carried the tea to the Market Square, which was located near where the monument stands today. They lit the crates on fire, which drew a crowd to the scene. Most of the village gathered around the fire as the perpetrators celebrated. McMahon writes, "When the fires died, the tea burners mounted their horses and with loud whoops raced down Greate Street and out of the village. There was no attempt to conceal identities. . . ."

The tea owners wanted restitution, and they came to Greenwich sheriff Jonathan Elmer for justice. Elmer's brothers, Ebenezer and Timothy, were a couple of the "Indians." Elmer picked a jury of relatives, friends, and political cohorts, who took the overwhelming evidence against the young men and voted there was "no cause for action."

New Jersey's governor, William Franklin, who sided with England in all American actions against the crown, realized the process had been corrupted by the sheriff. He picked a new prosecutor—Daniel Bowen, the man from whom the tea had been stolen. Bowen tried to rig the process the other way, but found he could not overcome the majority of patriot sympathizers. Again, the jury found "no cause for action," and the matter was dropped.

Two future governors were involved in the case. Tea burner Richard Howell was elected in 1793 and succeeded by the tea burners' attorney, Joseph Bloomfield, who took office in 1801 and for whom the town of Bloomfield is named. Ebenezer Elmer became a congressman, and his brother Timothy a member of the New Jersey Assembly. Joel Fithian, too, served in the New Jersey legislature.

The great tea-burning incident is remembered every year during the Christmas in Greenwich house tour (see Gibbon House) when a cannon-firing ceremony is held at the monument, Lest We Forget.

The Gibbon House

Ye Greate Street
Greenwich
(609) 455-4055

OPEN: Daily: NOON to 4 P.M. except Mondays. Sunday: 2 P.M. to 5 P.M. The Gibbon House is open from April 1 until the annual Christmas House Tour in early December, after which is closes for the winter. For information on the tour call the Gibbon House at the number listed above.

COST: Donations accepted.

DIRECTIONS: The house is well marked on Ye Greate Street. You can't miss it.

The Gibbon House is home to the well organized and publicity conscious Cumberland County Historical Society and a good place to start in exploring, not only Greenwich, but the area as a whole.

The house was built in 1730 by Nicholas Gibbon of Gravesend, England, a textile merchant who did business in the colonies.

The mansion, which features Flemish bond brickwork on the outside, is filled with artifacts from every period of Greenwich and Cumberland County history. Main attractions include the nine-foot colonial fireplace, where an authentic colonial meal is prepared by Mrs. Raginhild Holm each autumn during the town's annual Craft Faire (call Gibbon House for information), and a display of eighteen Ware chairs with ladder backs and rush seats.

Then there are the swords of the Potter family, a collection unique to Greenwich. It seems a Potter has served in nearly every United States conflict, and their individual sabres are displayed at the Gibbon House. The first belonged to David Potter, the first of the Potter's named David, who was a colonel with the Second Regiment of the Cumberland County Militia during the

Revolution. The seventh David Potter was a rear admiral in the United States Navy and served through World War I.

One thing is apparent after a visit to the Gibbon House. Greenwich is a proud little enclave, but not indifferent to outsiders, and the historical society is a driving force in community activities. The volunteers at the house are friendly and informative, and take time with visitors. They want people to come and learn their history and to attend no less than a dozen yearly events that celebrate it.

"We had four thousand people here for our last Craft Faire," said Mrs. Watson, the president of the historical society since 1968 and owner of The Griffin, an antiques and out-of-print book shop on the corner of Ye Greate Street and Sheppard's Mill Road. "We usually get about a thousand people for our Christmas tour."

Not bad for a town of a thousand.

The John DuBois Maritime Museum

The Greate Street

Greenwich

(609) 455-4055 (same as the Gibbon House)

OPEN: Beginning of April to end of October, Sundays: 1:30 P.M. to 4:30 P.M.

COST: Donation accepted.

DIRECTIONS: The DuBois museum is across the street and a few houses down from the Gibbon House. You can't miss it.

Octogenarian John DuBois lives in Absecon and operated a shipyard in Leesburg during the '30s and '40s. The museum is an 1852 building that was built as a Presbyterian lecture hall and has hosted Sunday school, Sons of the Revolution gatherings, and Grange meetings.

DuBois is a legendary South Jersey craftsman. When it came time for him to put his tools and artifacts in perpetuity, the choice was easy.

"He always wanted us (the Cumberland County Historical Society) to have (them)," Mrs. Watson said. "He's happy to have everything here in Greenwich."

The museum pays homage to the great shipbuilding industry and maritime traditions of the Delaware Bay. Outside is the bell from the old Ship John Lighthouse, that helped guide river pilots around a dangerous shoal in the bay. Inside are collections of shipbuilding tools and work benches, oyster traps, maps (including a map of the oyster grounds in the Maurice River), block and tackle displays, chisels and mallets, you name it.

There is a collection of ship half-models, including many made by Greenwich craftsman Robert Jackson, who lives near the museum with his wife, Ruth.

But most of the stuff belongs to DuBois, who once owned Mauricetown Shipyard on the Maurice River.

"He is the most knowledgeable person I've ever talked to about shipbuilding, oystering, coasting vessels . . . anything that has to do with the maritime traditions of this area," Mrs. Watson said.

DuBois began donating his collection a decade ago, and the museum opened in 1990.

"It was very important to him that these things had a permanent home," said Mrs. Watson. "That's how these traditions are kept alive."

The City of Bridgeton

TOURIST CENTER OPEN: Monday through Friday: 9 A.M. to 4 P.M. Saturdays, Sunday, and holidays: 10 A.M. to 4 P.M. The phone number for the Bridgeton-Cumberland Tourist Association is (609) 451-4802 or 455-3230 ext. 262.

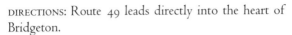

DIRECTIONS: Route 49 leads directly into the heart of Bridgeton.

Upriver from Greenwich on the meandering Cohansey River is Bridgeton, another town proud of its history. Bridgeton boasts the largest historic district in New Jersey, and maps are available at the town's Tourist Information Center at 50 East Broad Street (which is Route 49). The tourist center is in the old Pennsylvania Reading railroad station, so it's hard to miss.

Settlers came to Bridgeton in 1686, when Richard Hancock opened a sawmill on a tributary of the Cohansey now known as Mill Creek. In 1716 a bridge was built across the Cohansey, and the previously unnamed settlement grew to be called Cohansey Bridge. The bridge brought traffic—stage coaches and shipping wagons. Three taverns, owned by Silar Parvin, Elias Cotting, and William Doubleday open in 1716. Visitors from New York and Philadelphia would pass through, keeping the little settlement in touch with the big world. With the presence of the inns, Bridgeton became the place to be in Cumberland County, usurping the larger town of Greenwich. The town is an early example of a city forming around the country's primitive road network. Cumberland voters chose Cohansey Bridge over Greenwich as the county seat in 1749, much to the dismay of Greenwich residents.

In time the name Cohansey Bridge evolved into Bridge Town, then Bridgeton. A courthouse was built, and on July 7, 1776, the bell rang out from it's cupola to tell residents the colonies has declared independence three days earlier. That bell, known as Cumberland's Liberty Bell is on display at the current courthouse at the corner of Lafayette Street and West Broad (also Route 49).

Most of the historic homes in Bridgeton, however, are from a later period, when the town became one of the centers of South Jersey industry. From 1800 to 1838, the town's population exploded, going from 400 to 2,387. While there were only fifteen buildings in town in 1750, there were nearly five hundred by 1850, including four churches, four hotels, six blacksmith shops, seven tailors and seven shoemakers, twelve schools, a library, a brick courthouse, and a jail. Heavy industry also came to town: four lumber yards, a tin maker, a sheet-iron maker, a stove maker, a pump factory, a tannery, four carriage makers, a nail and iron factory, a wool mill, two grist mills, and a saw mill. Glassmaking became king after the Civil War.

The Cohansey began to see more action, too. Bridgeton became home port to a fleet of schooners and sloops that brought goods in and out of the growing city.

Bridgeton's historic homes reflect this industrial age and show a wide variety of architectural styles as American industrialists adopted European tastes. Some borrowed as much "taste" as they could squeeze into a mansion. A house on 137 Commerce St. has a French mansard roof, Italianate windows, a Greek revival front porch, a Colonial doorway, and overall Victorian charm. The house at 62-64 Bank St. has a Mediterranean center façade, flanked by two Victorian turrets. Of course, not everyone who lived in Bridgeton was a wealthy industrialist. Most of the people *worked* for the wealthy industrialists, and their homes are represented, too, like the four-walls-and-a-roof architectural example at 24 Franklin St.

Here are some other Bridgeton points of interest.

The Nail Mill Museum

Mayor Aitken Drive
Bridgeton City Park
(609) 455-4100

OPEN: April through December, Tuesday through Friday: 10:30 A.M. to 3:30 P.M. Saturdays and Sundays: 11 A.M. to 4 P.M.

COST: Free.

DIRECTIONS: From Route 49 in Bridgeton center head north on Route 697 (Atlantic Street), and follow it to the fork. Mayor Aitken Drive branches off to left.

The Nail Mill Museum pays homage to the Industrial Revolution in a building that was once the main office of the Cumberland Nail and Iron Company. Artifacts include tools and displays of early industry, photos and lithographs of old Bridgeton, and a display of ships from the 1800s in model form. There is also a collection of nineteenth-century toys, including model trains, and South Jersey's oldest public clock.

New Sweden Farmstead Museum

Mayor Aitken Drive
Bridgeton City Park
(609) 455-9785

OPEN: May through Labor Day. Wednesday to Saturday: 11 A.M. to 5 P.M. Sundays and holidays: NOON to 5 P.M.

COST: $3 for adults, $2.50 for seniors, $2 for students, $1.50 for children under 12, free for children under 6. Special $5 rate for families of four or larger.

DIRECTIONS: From Route 49 in Bridgeton center head north on Route 697 (Atlantic Street), and follow it to the fork. Mayor Aitken Drive branches off to left.

Before industry in Bridgeton, there were farm settlers. The Farmstead museum recreates seventeenth-century living, with a main house, a smokehouse, stable, barns, blacksmith shop, and the like.

The George Woodruff Indian Museum

> Bridgeton Public Library
> 150 East Commerce St.
> (609) 451-2620

OPEN: Monday through Saturday: 1 P.M. to 4 P.M. (except Saturdays in June, July, and August, when library closes at 1 P.M.) Or by appointment.

COST: Free.

DIRECTIONS: Commerce Street runs parallel with Route 49, 1 block north.

🐦 Before farmers settled in Bridgeton, there were Lenni-Lenape Indians. George Woodruff, who owned a local home heating-oil company, had a strong interest in Indian culture and collected over twenty thousand artifacts. Woodruff died about twenty years ago, and his collection was passed on to the town. It is housed in the library basement.

The Village of Fortescue

DIRECTIONS: Take Route 609 south off of Route 49 in Bridgeton, and follow it to Route 553 south in Fairton. Take Route 553 east (the Bridgeton–Port Norris Road) 8 miles to Route 656 south (Newport Landing Road). Go about 1 mile and find Route 637 south (Fortescue Road). This road leads directly to the village (about 5 miles). From Route 49 in Millville, take Route 610 west (the Cedarville-Millville Road) toward Centre Grove. At Centre Grove, bear left onto 629 south (the Newport-Centre Grove Road). This will join 656 south and take you to 637 south to Fortescue.

🐦 In the 1920s it was the Croaker Capital of the East Coast. Now it's known as the Weakfish Capital of the World.

Fish varieties come and go, but Fortescue remains.

"Without question, we're the recreational-fishing capital of the Delaware Bay," said Bunky Higbee, owner of Higbee's Marina on the island. "Anybody who sport fishes on the Delaware Bay knows about Fortescue."

Yes, Fortescue is an island, separated from the mainland by the narrow Fortescue Creek.

"People don't think of us as an island, but the fact is, you can take a boat and go in a circle around Fortescue," Higbee said.

The place certainly has the character of an island. There's one road in, the same road out. The road goes in a circle, making the rounds past the seven marinas in the village.

"Technically, they're not all marinas," Higbee said. "But everybody does something different. Borkowski's, for instance, rents rowboats to individual fishermen. Then we (Higbee's Marina) have the *Miss Fortescue,* a fifty-five-foot party boat, which is licensed to carry fifty people. We have thirty slips for small boats and a trailer launch. There's not that much competition between us down here, because we all offer something different. Everybody gets along real well. You have to do that to survive."

The best example of community cooperation is the State Marina at Fortescue. When the residents realized the state wasn't doing much to promote or maintain it, they pulled together and sub-leased it from the state.

"It's run by the Fortescue Captains and Boat Owners Association," Higbee said. "We operate it. We maintain it. We had to do it to keep it in business."

The weakfish, or the sea trout, is the headliner at Fortescue, followed by flounder, school bluefish and blue claw crabs.

"Around 1980 weakfish hit their peak," Higbee said. "Guys were going out and coming home with two or three coolers full. In 1980 you couldn't get a parking space in town if you got here late. The boats were almost always full. For some reason, there was a strong run on weakfish. Since then, it's gone progressively down a little every year. It's still good, but not as good as it was around 1980."

The reason?

"Everybody has an opinion. Everybody has their own whipping boy. Some say it's because of the (Salem) atomic plant. Some blame the commercial fishermen. Everybody blames everyone else but themselves. Me, I say we all over fished back in those days, and we're paying for it now."

While weakfish are still strong—it was Higbee and a few other long-timers who came up with the name the "Weakfish Capital of the World" few years ago—it was the croaker that put Fortescue on the map.

In the 1920s croakers were so plentiful that ten small hotels managed to stay in business on the island, putting up Philadelphians who came for a weekend of fishing. Higbee's maternal grandfather, who had a general store in Fortescue, also had a charter boat for croaker fishing.

The croakers were plentiful in the '20s, and again in the post–World War II years.

"Then the weakfish sort of took over," Higbee said.

Bunky Higbee is the third generation of Fortescue fishing-business entrepreneurs. His father, who came from a long line of farmers, decided he liked the hard work of the bay more than the hard work inland, and he joined his father-in-law in Fortescue.

Today, Bunky Higbee's entire family is in the Fortescue business. His oldest son, Jim, captains *Miss Fortescue.* His middle son, Cliff, runs the bait-and-tackle shop. His youngest son, Charles, helps run the marina. His wife, Betty, and daughter, Cindy, run the restaurant.

While business isn't bad, it could be better. Higbee wishes he could attract more off-season trade.

"Almost everyone opens in the first week of May and closes after Columbus Day weekend," he said. "We don't close because there's no fish, we close because there's no people. There's plenty of fishing, but television's got everybody convinced summer ends on Labor Day. It got to the point were we'd get so few people, it wasn't worth staying open."

The Down Jersey Folklife Center

Wheaton Village
1501 Glasstown Road
Millville
(609) 825-6800 or (800) 998-4552

OPEN: Wheaton Village is open daily: 10 A.M. to 5 P.M., except Easter, Thanksgiving, and Christmas. Folklife Center hours vary slightly, so call ahead.

COST: The Folklife Center is free with paid admission to the village. Wheaton Village prices are $6 for adults, $5.50 for seniors, and $3.50 for students. Children 5 and under are free, and there is a special $12 admission price for families.

DIRECTIONS: Wheaton is well-marked and can be reached by taking Exit 26 on Route 55, or finding Wade Boulevard off Route 49 (at the eastern end of Millville. Take Wade Boulevard north and follow the signs to Wheaton.

The Down Jersey Folklife Center, which opened in September of 1994, is located in Wheaton Village. The village is more or less devoted to glass. There is a Museum of American Glass, which has over seven thousand items from early Mason jars, which were invented in 1858 by tinsmith John Mason in Vineland, to up-to-date fiber-optics components. The replica 1888 glass factory of Wheaton Industries is a living monument to a dying craft, and visitors can watch gaffers (glass blowers) shape and mold bottles, pitchers, vases, et cetera. The Creative Glass Center of America shows what artistic hands can make from glass.

Glassmaking was South Jersey's most widespread industry/

craft. Glassboro, Vineland, Bridgeton, Salem, and Millville were glassmaking centers.

Of course, there are other crafts unique to South Jersey, many of which have become part of the region's maritime traditions. The Down Jersey Folklife Center has collected examples of these crafts.

The center focuses on the crafts and folk art of New Jersey's bottom eight counties—Atlantic, Burlington, Camden, Cape May, Cumberland, Glouchester, Ocean, and Salem. Many of the artists and craftsmen represented at the folklife center are legends in South Jersey.

Tom Brown of Millville is a fur trapper. The octogenarian the last survivor of an industry that was prevalent in the area for three hundred years.

Barbara Fiedler of Pleasantville makes coiled pine needle baskets.

The late Alexander Gustavis had a basket shop in Vineland and is South Jersey's best known basketmaker. The late Noah Newcomb of Dividing Creek, another basket legend, is also represented at the center.

John Dubois (see John DuBois Maritime Museum, *Salem*

Examples of this New Jersey skiff along with other traditional South Jersey crafts can be seen at the Folklife Center in Wheaton Village.

County) is a noted boat builder, an oyster-boat captain, and shipyard owner, who may possess more working knowledge of South Jersey maritime life than any man alive.

Charlie Hankins made the Sea Bright skiff, a fishing/lifeguard boat designed to pound through surf. Charlie Hankins learned this business from his father and ran a shop in Lavalette for nearly fifty years before retiring.

John Van Duyne of Linwood was the first person to make a surf boat out of fiberglass, and his boats are used by lifeguard crews throughout the coast.

For folklife center director Jack Shortlidge, the researching of South Jersey crafts and folk art has been an education.

"It was a revelation because I had that midwestern stereotype of New Jersey as just being an extension of New York," said Shortlidge, who is from Columbus, Ohio. "I studied folklore in school, so I was aware of New Jersey to the extent of what some other folklorists had written about, but I think its underplayed. Obviously, we're trying to change that."

Many of the displays at the folklife center focus on maritime traditions and wildlife. Noah Newcomb's baskets were made for the oystermen on the Delaware Bay. Bob Seabrook has a collection of oyster cans, which look like paint cans, on display. James Boyce is a wood carver who specializes in terns and ducks. There are old photographs of the Hankins and Van Duyne shops, and displays of old tools for boat building, and equipment for harvesting sea and bay creatures.

"This center is about people, not products," said Shortlidge. "These crafts, their work, goes to the very essence of who they are."

Mauricetown

DIRECTIONS: Take Route 47 to Route 670 west, and follow over the bridge into the heart of Mauricetown.

Like Greenwich, Mauricetown is one of New Jersey's best kept secrets. From the top of the bridge leading into town from Route 47, you get a quick panoramic glimpse of what's ahead: a ten-block village loaded with Victorian, Georgian, and gothic-revival homes.

From the bridge top, Mauricetown looks like a thriving little resort town; many of the homes are large enough to be bed-and-breakfast inns, and there are a number of impressive pleasure boats docked in the river.

But on a Saturday morning in August, you have a lot less trouble getting into Mauricetown than, say, Cape May. All the more reason to come, says Irene Ferguson, a lifelong resident and head of the Mauricetown Historical Society.

"We only have about four hundred people in town, and, we have annual events to attract people—like our Christmas House

Mauricetown dresses up for the annual Christmas tour of the vintage homes.

JOHN DI IONNO

A captain's home in Mauricetown.

tour, which usually draws about a thousand, and the fire department's Seafood Festival in the fall, which is for two days and brings lots and lots of people to town—but I wouldn't say we have a tourist trade. We don't even have a restaurant in town, I'm sorry to say. I wish we did."

What Mauricetown does have is seven antique shops and enough restored homes and historical homes to make it a great walking-around town. It's also a place so unknown, you can feel as if you're in on some wonderful secret.

"That's what we are . . . just a very quiet little town," Ferguson said.

It wasn't always that way. In the latter part of the nineteenth century and the first few years of the twentieth, Mauricetown was a busy shipping and shipbuilding port. It's beautiful homes, most of which are still standing, were built by sea captains. If Fortescue can call itself the "Weakfish Capital of the World" and if Port Norris was once the "Oyster Capital of the World," certainly Mauricetown can grab the less grandiose title of "Sea Captain Capital of Cumberland County."

Mauricetown was home to eighty-nine sea captains between

1846 and 1915, the best years of shipping and shipbuilding on the Maurice River. The shipyards specialized in oyster boats, coastal schooners, and barge-type boats to carry the cordwood and cedar logs that were plentiful in the area. The captains ran cargo up and down the Atlantic coast, from Newfoundland to South America.

At the Mauricetown Episcopal Church on Noble Street, a stained-glass window installed in 1921 memorializes the twenty-two captains from Mauricetown who died at sea. Obviously, this was dangerous work, with roughly one-fourth of all captains going down with their ships.

Mauricetown plays up it's maritime history and many of the captains' homes are marked by plaques.

On Front Street, which runs parallel with the river, you find the former homes of Capt. Maurice Godfrey, Capt. Isaac Peterson, Capt. Charles Sharp, Capt. Samuel Sharp, and Capt. John Sharp, Jr.

Capt. John Sharp, Sr., had his home on High Street—the main road in town—as did Capt. Alfred Haley, Capt. Charles Buckaloo, and Capt. Abel Haley (is that a classic name for a sailing ship captain or what?)

Capt. Jorge Weaver lived on Second Street, Capt. William Haley over on Mauricetown-Buckshutem Road.

If you're noticing a certain repetition of names, that's because the sea life, as they say, gets in the blood. But the biggest name on the Mauricetown historical home circuit belongs to the Comptons, the family name of the three New England brothers who came to Mauricetown in 1810.

All three brothers had homes built for them on Front Street by Flagg Bacon, a builder who came down with them from New England. Ichabod Compton's home was built in 1812—the mansard roof was added 80 years later—and is still one of the most impressive in town.

Another architectural attraction is the Caesar Hoskins Swedish Log Cabin, at the corner of South and Second Streets. The home has been modified to accommodate twentieth-century living, but the early part (ca. 1600–1650) is clearly visible.

Irene Ferguson, who lives in the Capt. Alfred Haley house and has an antique shop out back called The Cookhouse, started the historical society thirteen years ago to preserve the rich maritime history of the town.

"We've always had a lot of pride. The one thing we didn't have was money," she said.

The pride is evident in the historical society's membership, which numbers one hundred fifteen. Not bad for a town of four hundred.

"Some of the people do come from out of town," Ferguson said, "but we do have an active group."

Eleven years ago, the group bought the Edward Compton house, a decaying Italianate Victorian mansion. They've been restoring it ever since, to convert it into the Mauricetown Historical Society Museum.

"When we started, people didn't think we'd make it, but we did it. We did it with hard work and money raised at cake sales, fudge sales, craft shows, every kind of sale imaginable," Ferguson said. "We're just starting to get our collection together, and we're going to have a library with local information and local genealogy."

The museum is located on Front Street (there are no street numbers in Mauricetown) and for now is open by appointment. The phone number is (609) 785-0457.

"Tell them to call, and if they want to see it, one us will run over and open it up for them." Ferguson said.

The Port Norris, Bivalve, and Shellpile Area

DIRECTIONS: From Mauricetown, take Route 744 west to Route 649 south, and follow it 3 miles into Port Norris center. Make a right on to Route 553, and go 1 block to find the Schooner Center (see below). There are three left-hand turns off of Route 553 that will take you to Bivalve and Shellpile—Ogden Avenue, High Street, and Memorial Avenue. All three will take you to the Maurice River wharf area, where they basically merge.

It was called the Oyster Capital of the World. The oyster beds of the Delaware Bay were once so full that there were twenty-nine processing plants and shipping companies in the Port Norris area of the Maurice River. Now there is one big one. Fifty years ago, there were five hundred oyster boats working in the area. Now, a few long-timers hold on. There were one hundred-car freight trains, heading north with the daily harvest. Now the only whistle you hear is the wind through the marsh grass.

The main culprit in the slow death of the oyster industry was a traumatic event almost four decades ago. A disease known as MSX hit the beds, and, almost overnight, the Port Norris oyster industry went from a healthy six-million-dollar-a-year business employing forty-five hundred people, to a barely breathing business that could support no more than a few companies and a few family-run boats.

The industry never fully recovered from the MSX episode, and other factors have compounded the problem over the years: pollution in the Delaware Bay, government warnings on oyster consumption, re-occurring oyster diseases that wiped out all mature oysters as recently as 1991, environmental laws, boat insurance.

The only continuously active packing company at Port Norris is Bivalve Packing, with two others intermittently opening, then suspending operations. Many of the surviving fishing families have adjusted to the dearth of oysters. John R. (Bobby) Bateman II comes from an oystering family—one of the Bivalve Packing boats is named after his grandfather—but today Bateman runs a crabbing business on High Street in Bivalve. His two boats go out each morning before dawn and return in midafternoon. Bateman is mostly in the wholesale business, simply because there aren't that many retail customers in the area.

Despite the fall-off of the oyster trade, the Port Norris-Bivalve-Shellpile is still an interesting place to visit. Like Belford in Monmouth County (see *Monmouth County*) this is an authentic fishing village. You can go down to the waterfront and see oyster boats, mountains of crab traps, and flocks of sea-gulls picking through piles of shells.

The wharf area is home to the Rutgers Oyster Research Laboratory, the remaining oyster processing plants, and a few marinas. But in the next few years it will also be the home base of the Delaware Bay Schooner Center.

The Delaware Bay Schooner Project
Exhibit: **Maritime Traditions of the Delaware Bay**

> 18 E. Main St.
> Port Norris
> Office and *A. J. Meerwald*
> 48 Shell Rd.
> Bivalve
> (609) 785-2060

OPEN: April to October, Saturdays and Sundays: 1 P.M. to 4:30 P.M. Otherwise by appointment.

COST: Donations accepted.

DIRECTIONS: Route 553 is Main Street in Port Norris and the permanent exhibit of the Delaware Bay Schooner Project is near the center of town in a two-story building.

NOTE: The Maritime Center plans to move to the wharf area of Bivalve on High Street, about 1 mile from its current location in the near future.

The Schooner Project's permanent exhibit, Maritime Traditions of the Delaware Bay, is only a few years old, but it has the look of an old-time mariner's attic. There's a little of everything about the Delaware Bay, from oil paintings of schooners to antique tools. The Schooner Project's collection is crammed into a small storefront. Visitors squeeze through the rows of artifacts and information, which are set up like aisles in an old, wood-floored 5 & 10.

The exhibits on shipping, oystering, commercial fishing, and recreational uses of the Delaware Bay, and the trades that evolved in the area include the tools of local sailmaking legend Ed Cobb, the workbench of oyster basketmaker Noah Newcomb (see Down Jersey Folklife Center), and many historic photographs from the John DuBois collection (see John DuBois Maritime Museum in Greenwich).

The project's artifacts, new and old, don't wander too far from home. The focus remains on the Port Norris area. There is a big model ship called the *Charles H. Stowman*, which was never a real ship, just the big model built for and named after the owner of the Stowman Boat Yard in Dorchester, called the Dorchester Shipyard today. There is a sixteen-foot by four-foot mural called *Maritime Traditions* by local artist Glenn Rudderow.

The Maritime Traditions exhibit may look like a mom-and-pop museum, but it is not. It's a well-planned and financed project, aimed at restoring the area's heritage. A resource center is underway, and the entire Delaware Bay Schooner Project will have a new home in the Bivalve wharf area in the next few years.

Each year the project staffers organize Delaware Bay Day, which is basically like any other community fair in the area but with a few unique touches: a maritime landscape bus tour takes visitors to historic and significant sites in the area, a lecture series focuses on bay-related issues, there is a fleet parade up the Maurice River, and an oyster shucking contest. Call (609) 785-2060 for more information.

The exhibit in Port Norris is just one part of the Delaware Bay Schooner Project, which is centered around the restoration of a dead-in-the-water oyster schooner named the *Clyde A. Phillips* to its original state, when it was built as the *A. J. Meerwald* in 1928.

The executive director of the Schooner Project is Meghan Wren of Dorchester, who grew up in Millville and worked in boat yards in Greenwich and Dorchester.

In 1988 she was working with a local boat owner named John Gandy, who was planning to restore the *Phillips,* which was deteriorating in the Maurice River at Mauricetown. The plans fell through, and Wren, then twenty-three, decided to take a shot at it herself.

Launching of the new A. J. Meerwald, *September 12, 1995.*

The A. J. Meerwald, circa 1930. Courtesy of Delaware Bay Schooner Project.

"Everything was moving very slowly until the boat sank," she said. "Believe it or not, that was the best thing that happened to us. It sped up the process. . . . It made people realize this boat was close to being lost and it needed to be restored."

With the help of many local volunteer fire companies, the boat was pumped out, raised, and towed down river to Bivalve in early 1993. It was hoisted out of the water by a crane and put down in scaffolding built for the restoration. A group of professional shipwrights and volunteers started working as Wren lined up grants and other funding.

In September of 1995 the hull was completed and the boat was launched into the Maurice River at Bivalve. The work was not yet completed: the rigging had to be done; the engine, plumbing, the bilge pumps, and electrical systems had to be put in; and the passenger and crew accommodations had to be built. The final tally was close to six hundred and fifty thousand dollars raised by grants and donations.

The *Meerwald* is used for educational purposes, taking school groups and other day-trippers out of ports from Trenton to Lewes, Delaware, on the Bay side and also on the Atlantic coast.

"The whole purpose is to use the schooner to raise awareness of the Delaware estuary and how it has shaped the culture and history of this region," said Jean Walat, the educational director of the Schooner Project.

Bivalve will continue to be the *Meerwald*'s home base, and it will be the main attraction on the 140-foot wharf-front property the Schooner Project will soon be calling home. (note: Call (609) 785-2060 for a copy of the boat's schedule or other information on the Delaware Bay Schooner Project and its exhibits.)

The East Point Lighthouse

End of East Point Road
Heislerville
(609) 476-4532

OPEN: Under renovation, but exterior may be viewed at all times. The group trying to save the lighthouse, the Maurice River Historical Society, also holds an annual open house in August and may open the lighthouse on request. Call (609) 476-4532 for further information.

COST: Donations accepted.

DIRECTIONS: Take Route 49 to Route 47 south in Millville, which runs parallel with the Maurice River. Follow the signs at Route 616 south to Dorchester, Leesburg, and Heislerville. At Heislerville (about 6 miles from Route 47 at Millville) make a right onto East Point Road, and follow it to the lighthouse.

A map in a little general store in the West Texas Badlands tells visitors, "You are here. In the middle of absolutely nowhere."

At first glance, this seems to apply to the East Point Lighthouse, too. The lighthouse may be the most desolate place in

New Jersey, the nation's most densely populated state. And instead of the cattle skulls seen littering the desert floor of the Badlands, visitors to East Point will find the empty shells of horseshoe crabs scattered along the beach. Interestingly, after beer and soda cans, the most visible man-made litter in the area is lost ball caps.

In addition to being the most desolate place in New Jersey, East Point may also have the strongest winds, except for maybe the jet-propelled gusts on runways at Newark Airport. Even the occasional fisherman who visits East Point in summer is outfitted in long pants, a windbreaker, and a hat, battened-down to keep his hair from blowing away. Late autumn and early spring fisherman dress more like the ice fisherman you'd see on a Sussex County lake in February.

None of this, however, should dissuade you from visiting East Point.

The beach around it is full of waterfowl, horseshoe crabs migrate through there in May and June, and bay turtles come there to lay eggs.

The lighthouse also has enough historical relevance to be included on both the state and national historic registers.

But more than anything else, it's the peace. It's not often you get to experience solitude like this in New Jersey. It's hard to believe that for nearly one hundred years there was lightkeeper stationed there. Out there. Alone. Every day and every night.

"It certainly wasn't a choice duty station," said Jim Gowdy, a New Jersey lighthouse aficionado and vice-president of the Maurice River Historical Society. "It wasn't the worst, but it was far from the best. The road to the lighthouse often flooded and there was no electricity out there, but eleven different keepers, and presumably their families, made it work."

The lighthouse is the second oldest surviving beacon in New Jersey, after Sandy Hook (see Sandy Hook, *Monmouth County*). Built in 1849 the Cape Cod–style lighthouse guided river pilots, fishermen, oystermen, and other boaters into the mouth of the Maurice River for ninety-two consecutive years, when it was deactivated—for the first time—in 1941 by the U.S. Coast Guard.

East Point, called the Maurice River Lighthouse until 1913, is working today. The Coast Guard reactivated it in 1980, and an automated electric beam now shines over the Maurice River inlet every night.

"It is very unusual for a lighthouse to be reactivated," Gowdy said. "Once they go dark, usually that's it."

The East Point Lighthouse is the last working navigational beam on the New Jersey side of the Delaware Bay. And it's a miracle it made it this far.

After the lighthouse was shut down in 1941, it was neglected by all except groups of vandals who, because of its isolation, made it a favorite target. The New Jersey Division of Fish, Game, and Wildlife took over the property in 1956, mainly for its access to the bay. The vandalism continued, and the wear

The East Point Lighthouse has taken a beating over the years, from nature and vandals, but a restoration project is underway.

and tear from the harsh weather left the lighthouse, well, worn and torn. In 1971 a group of citizens formed the Maurice River Historical Society in order to save the lighthouse. They weren't a moment to soon. Shortly after the group formed, a fire set by vandals devastated the building: the lantern room was destroyed, so was the attic area and most of the upper floor and roof.

Fish and Game was leaning toward knocking it down. The historical group lobbied hard to keep it, raising funds and volunteers to do the repairs. They leased it from the state and in the ensuing years the group was able to repair the damage and cover the windows to keep out the wind, rain, and miscreants. Still, the building wasn't out of danger. Stabilizing such an old structure in such a fierce environment is next to impossible and, to this day, the group is working against long odds to save the lighthouse.

"Even when the Coast Guard reactivated it we still had responsibility for the building," Gowdy said. "All they own is the electric line and lamp. If something happened to the building, they'd take their electricity and go home. Fixing the building is totally up to us."

The vandalism has slowed since a cottage was moved to the property and rented. The building has improved and the group has built a numbers of walkways and stairs to give visitors better access. A federal grant will help with the next stage of rehabilitation, although money and volunteers are always in short supply.

"We've improved the signage so at least people know it's there," Gowdy said. "And people come. From all over. I was working there one day and a couple of people drove up. They came from Virginia to see it. A few hours later, I got a few more people from New Jersey. People who know about lighthouses know about this one."

Salem County

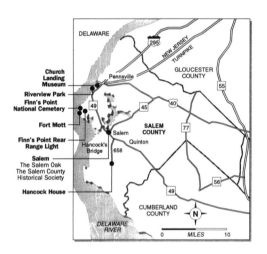

DELAWARE

295
NEW JERSEY TURNPIKE

Church Landing Museum

Pennsville

GLOUCESTER COUNTY

55

Riverview Park

Finn's Point National Cemetery

49

45

40

Fort Mott

SALEM COUNTY

77

Finn's Point Rear Range Light

Salem

Salem
The Salem Oak
The Salem County
Historical Society

Hancock's Bridge

Quinton

658

56

Hancock House

49

CUMBERLAND COUNTY

N

DELAWARE RIVER

0   MILES   10

Best reached by the New Jersey Turnpike, the interior of Salem County is a far cry from the industrial centers of the Delaware near Philadelphia. There is a strong culture in the county, and the river runs quietly alongside a number of recreation areas and historical sites throughout the county. Salem has some of the best examples of eighteenth- and nineteenth-century architecture in the state. The historical society can furnish maps and descriptions of many of the well-preserved landmarks. Of course, there is a country side to Salem, too. Agriculture is as big now as it was when the H. J. Heinz Company opened a packing plant there. Farmer's markets line every major road, and the Cowtown Rodeo in Woodstown, one of only two professional rodeos in the Northeast, continues to draw crows on weekends.

Church Landing Museum

86 Church Landing Road
Pennsville
(609) 678-4453

OPEN: Wednesdays and Sundays: NOON to 4 P.M.

COST: Tours of museum are $2, $1 for seniors.

DIRECTIONS: Church Landing Road is off Route 49 in Pennsville, just 2 miles south of the New Jersey Turnpike. Looks for signs, and the small, brick St. John's Episcopal Church on the corner. Follow Church Landing Road almost to its end. The driveway for the museum is the second to the last turn on right. (The last turn is a private home).

The Church Landing Museum is in a classic Gothic-American farmhouse, right up to the wood roof shingles. The house, which is home to the Pennsville Historical Society, has been restored and furnished to look as it did in 1860, the year it was built. Inside are an assortment of period furniture and clothing. Outside are an old-fashioned laundry room and an outhouse. But what makes this place special are the grounds. The house sits a hundred yards from the Delaware River, in the shadow of the Delaware Memorial Bridge, and yet it is covered with shade trees and gardens. There is a riverside gazebo and a dozen park benches and picnic benches spread around the grounds. It is so quiet, you can actually hear the river flowing.

The area marks the spot of a boat launch in Penns Neck, where early Finnish and Swedish settlers would gather on Sunday mornings for a trip, up river and against the current, to Wilmington to attend church. In time they decided it was easier to build their own church than continue the risky trip across the Delaware.

While the settlers abandoned their weekly sojourn across the Delaware, ferries ran on the river in more recent times, up until 1952, when the Delaware Memorial Bridge was built. The big bridge killed the ferry lines, but the historical society has a little piece of the ferry boat history in the yard of the farmhouse—a life boat under restoration.

The farmhouse was built around 1860 by Daniel and Rebecca Garrison. The Daniel Garrison who built the home was the fourth Daniel Garrison to own the land. The first Daniel Garrison bought the land in 1740. The land passed on to Daniel Garrison's for five generations, when the sixth generation Daniel Garrison broke the chain by turning the homestead down. It passed to his sister, Josephine, and her husband, whose last name was Locuson. Josephine Locuson's daughter, Anna, was the last of the Garrisons to own the home. When she died a few years ago, the land was bought by Atlantic Electric, leased to the historical society, and restored as a joint venture between the big-utility and the small-town preservationists.

Riverview Park

Route 49
Pennsville

OPEN: DAWN TO DUSK

COST: Free

DIRECTIONS: Follow Route 49 east from the New Jersey Turnpike, about 4 miles.

The entrance to Riverview Park catches your eye. It's a towering, wooden lattice structure, painted green with white letters. It looks Victorian. It looks festive, like the entrance to an old-time amusement park. In fact, the big façade is all that remains of one New Jersey's great waterfront amusement parks.

In its heyday, Riverview Beach Park drew customers from all over the bay, including many who arrived by ferry from Philadelphia, Chester, Pennsylvania, and Wilmington, Delaware.

The fun started at Riverview back in 1888, when local farmers decided to hold an annual picnic there. The next year a merry-go-round was brought in. The land was used for casual recreation until 1917, when owner W. D. Acton built and opened Riverview Beach Park, a state-of-the-art amusement park. The amusement park was eventually sold to the Wilson Line Company, which operated the ferries that brought customers there. In 1967 the park, showing signs of it's half-century of operation, was closed, and all the rides were auctioned off. The façade, however, remained. In 1976 the town bought the park and made it a public park.

The expansive park has a dirt running track and three big playgrounds for kids. Along the river there are a number of gazebos and covered porches, and a series of free-standing bench swings, for those who want to just sit and watch the water roll by. The tradition of the annual farmer's picnic continues. Each year, on the weekend after Labor Day, the park hosts Septemberfest, Pennsville's annual town fair.

Finns Point Rear Range Light

Fort Mott and Lighthouse Roads
Salem

OPEN: Tower can be viewed at all times, but is open for touring April through October, the third Sunday of every month: NOON to 4 P.M.

COST: Donations accepted.

DIRECTIONS: Follow Route 49 east from the New Jersey Turnpike about 4 miles, looks for signs for Fort Mott State Park. Make a right onto Fort Mott Road, and follow it south toward the park. The Rear Range Light will be in a big clearing, at the intersection of Fort Mott and Lighthouse Roads. Because of it's size, it is impossible to miss.

The Rear Range Light was part of a two-light system in the Fort Mott area, which helped river pilots navigate the tricky Delaware channel. The 115-foot tower worked in concert with the front light, which was actually in Fort Mott. Captains would move up or down the river, watching for the lights from the shore to become aligned. When that happened they knew to make a hard turn in the river. The wrought-iron lighthouse was built in 1876 at a cost of twelve hundred dollars, about the cost of a section of wrought-iron fence today, uninstalled. There was a keeper's cottage at the base, and the keeper had to climb the 119-step spiral staircase, then an 11-foot ladder to the lantern room to light the 150,000-candlepower kerosene vapor lamp at night and extinguish it in the morning.

The first keeper was a fellow named Thomas Dickinson, who was paid five hundred dollars a year. Dickinson held the job until 1907, when his wife took over. In all, there were only four keepers in the light's fifty-six-year history of manned operation, and Mrs. Dickinson only held the job for a year. The last lightkeeper was Milton Duffield, who climbed the stairs from 1916 until 1933, when the light was shut down.

A year later, river pilots, who missed its guidance, petitioned the government to reactivate it. The light was automated and continued that way from 1934 until 1950.

The keeper's house was vandalized and burned repeatedly until it was demolished in 1977. Area residents felt it was just a matter of time before the lighthouse was gone too, so a Save the Lighthouse Committee was formed. The lighthouse was placed on the National Register of Historic Places and the U.S. Fish and Wildlife Service came up with $33,600 to repair and restore it. It was re-opened to the public in 1984.

The lighthouse is actually part of the Supawna Meadows National Wildlife Refuge. It is not unusual to see sandpipers scurrying around the property, or egrets circling—egrets have

The Rear Range Light at Finn's Point.

a habit of following grass-cutting tractors on nearby farms. Unlike the Great Swamp National Wildlife Refuge in Chatham Township or the Edwin B. Forsythe at Brigantine (see *Ocean County*), Supawna has virtually no public access, except for the occasional deer and waterfowl hunts. The twenty-five hundred-acre refuge is about 75 percent marshland and an important stop for migrating and wintering waterfowl.

Fort Mott State Park

Fort Mott Road
Salem
(609) 935-3218

OPEN: DAWN TO DUSK.

COST: Free.

DIRECTIONS: Follow Route 49 east from the New Jersey Turnpike about 4 miles, look for signs for Fort Mott. Make a right onto Fort Mott Road, and follow it to the park entrance.

Fort Mott was New Jersey's second concrete fortification, the first being Fort Hancock at Sandy Hook (see *Monmouth County*), which defended the New York Harbor. Fort Mott's job was to shell any enemy that entertained thoughts of steaming into the Delaware Bay, then up the river to attack Philadelphia.

Like Sandy Hook, Fort Mott was part of the United States's post–Civil War military build-up. The build-up of European navys—who maybe thought the United States was vulnerable after the deadly internal war—called for new fortifications. The leap in warfare technology that occurred during the Civil War meant new fortifications had to be bigger, stronger, and have more firepower than ever.

Construction of Fort Mott began in 1872, but after four years only two of eleven planned gun emplacements were built.

From 1876 to 1896 there was no additional work done at the fort. But with the Spanish-American War looming, the government "re-emphasized" Fort Mott. Big, retractable guns were brought in and put behind concrete barriers. Like the later guns at Sandy Hook, the Fort Mott guns worked with counter-weights. The counterweight, when unleashed, would swing the gun to the surface for firing. The recoil from firing would swing the guns underneath the concrete barrier, where they would be re-loaded. Fort Mott had three, ten-inch guns and three, twelve-inch guns, which were capable of hurling thousand-pound shells between seven and eight miles. Smaller rapid fire guns were put in too for close range action, specifically to defend the seawalls of the riverfront Fort.

Fort Mott, which was obsolete by World War I and closed down as a military installation in 1922, never fired a shot in anger. But some of the nonmilitary history of the Fort is pretty interesting. For instance, the damp underground caverns and passageways where ammunition was transported and stored and the guns were loaded, posed a particular problem for soldiers,

MARK DI IONNO

Abandoned gun batteries at Fort Mott were once leased to mushroom growers.

who had to keep the gunpowder dry. If the gunpowder got wet, soldiers would then have to "dry" it, which required handling and heating it much more than they wanted (no wonder the most common nickname for Fort Mott soldiers was "Stumpy" . . . just kidding.). But for mushroom farmers, it was a perfect environment. For a time, the government leased the former gun batteries to mushroom growers, who used the dank area as a kind of greenhouse.

Also, there is a strip of Fort Mott that juts into the Delaware River which, because of the way state boundaries are drawn, is actually part of the state of Delaware

A great question for New Jersey trivia nuts: What are the only two states you can get to from New Jersey without crossing water? New York and Delaware. Of course, the answer needs an explanation.

For years, this strip of Delaware was a favorite spot for teenage drinking parties, because New Jersey state park rangers and police and local police had no jurisdiction. It got to be such a problem that the Delaware legislature had to pass a bill, granting the New Jersey police powers on the strip.

The park sits on the river, and walking along the raised concrete fortifications enhances the view. From the banks of Fort Mott you can see Fort Delaware on Pea Patch Island (see Finn's Point National Cemetery) and the rising banks of the Delaware side of the river. The low, flat riverbanks at Fort Mott and the flowing river air currents make it perfect place for kite-flying, a favorite pastime of Fort Mott visitors.

There is very little shade at Fort Mott—trees have a way of slowing down cannonballs—so it can become extremely uncomfortable on hot days. On those brutal, 95-degree, 95-percent humidity days we have all too frequently here in New Jersey, plan to visit the Fort in the early morning or late afternoon.

Also at the fort is a New Jersey Coastal Heritage Trail

Welcome Center, which has a small museum, including photographs and artifacts of old-time industry and recreation along the coast, and informational brochures. Call (609) 935-3218 for hours.

Finn's Point National Cemetery

Adjacent to Fort Mott

The Union prison at Fort Delaware on Pea Patch Island in the Delaware River off Fort Mott was a living hell for Confederate soldiers. The island prison was always damp. Diseases ran rampant through the twelve thousand men who were crammed into a jail designed to hold no more than four thousand. The prisoners from Gettysburg numbered 2,400 alone. A dysentery epidemic ran through the population, killing twenty men a day. The filth attracted such a proliferation of bugs and rodents that Dr. S. Weir Mitchell of Philadelphia wrote that sick prisoners "have more life on them than in them."

The Union soldiers who worked as prison guards were not immunized by uniform color: many of them, too, got sick and died.

The Confederate dead were transported, in open barges, to a low-lying area on the Jersey side of the Delaware at Finn's Point and dumped into mass graves. In all, 2,700 confederate Southerners died at Fort Delaware and 2,436 are buried at Finn's Point. The small number of Union soldiers who died at Fort Delaware were given proper burials and grave markers.

By 1875 the graveyard was overrun and neglected, the U.S. Army was asked by a number of southern governors to make the site a national cemetery.

They did, but to add insult to injury, the federal government authorized a monument to the Union dead in 1879.

It wasn't until 1910 that the rebels got their monument: an eighty-five-foot tower made of Pennsylvania granite.

The monument to the Confederate dead at Finn's Point National Cemetery.

With it's national cemetery status, Finn's Point also became the final resting place for a number of veterans from the Spanish-American War and World War I. There are also the graves of thirteen German prisoners, who died at Fort Dix during World War II.

The cemetery today is impeccably maintained, and one of the quietest places you will ever visit. On days when there is no wind and the leaves are still, there is nothing but the silence of the dead; the horrors they endured have been muted by time.

Salem City

DIRECTIONS: Take the New Jersey Turnpike to below Exit 1. After paying toll, look for signs for Route 49 east. Follow Route 49 east into the heart of Salem.

Trenton, Morristown, Elizabeth, New Brunswick, Princeton . . . these are the New Jersey towns that first come to mind when Colonial history is the topic. Salem belongs on the

J. GAYNER

The Salem port is making a comeback.

same list. The first English port in New Jersey was here, predating the port at Philadelphia. The port is now undergoing an extensive rehabilitation to make it more competitive in today's shipping market.

Not only was Salem settled by English colonists before the aforementioned towns, it also hosted its share of bloody Revolutionary War action.

It is a town of legend: agriculturist Robert Gibbon Johnson is said to have eaten a tomato in front of a large crowd in July of 1820, thereby proving that the red fruit was not poisonous and launching New Jersey's tomato industry.

It is a town of world and national renown: the acorns of the Salem Oak have been sown worldwide with hopes that they will produce an equally enduring and mighty tree, just as the name Salem was promulgated by the Street family from coast to coast. The Streets left Salem in 1803, when repeated crop failures caused by soil depletion forced many farming families to head west. Zadock Street founded Salem, Ohio, then pushed west and founded Salem, Indiana. His son, Aaron, pushed further, and founded Salem, Iowa, and finally, Salem, Oregon.

Salem is a town proud of its history. Each year on the last Saturday in August, the town celebrates its history on Market Street Day with historic house and church tours, food and entertainment, including a Robert Gibbon Johnson Tomato Eating Skit at the Old Court House. Each December many historic homes are opened for a tour (call the Salem County Historical Society at (609) 935-5004 for information.)

Points of interest in Salem include; the First Presbyterian Church (88 Market St.) with its towering white steeple, it is one of the prettiest churches you'll see anywhere; the old Salem Courthouse (Market Street and Broadway), a Georgian Colonial building that dates back to 1735, although it was rebuilt in 1817; and the Salem Friends Meeting House (East Broadway), which was built in 1772 and houses the state's most enduring church service group. The Friends have been meeting here since the days of John Fenwick (see below).

The Salem Oak

Friends Cemetery, Route 49 (Broadway)

DIRECTIONS: Take Route 49 into the heart of Salem, where the highway is named Broadway. Across the street from the Salem Oak Diner is the big tree. It stands near the opening in the cemetery wall.

New Jersey's most famous tree sits near the entrance of the Friends Cemetery. The tree was part of the original forest that covered the land when John Fenwick and a group of English settlers came ashore off the Delaware River in 1675 and began laying out a town along a feeder tributary, now known as the Salem River. Salem founder Fenwick was said to have stood in its shade when he signed a treaty with the Indians, shortly after arriving, gaining their trust with guns, liquor, clothing, and the usual assortment of knickknacks.

The Salem Oak Diner, a survivor from another era, just like the big tree across the street.

Fenwick did not actually buy the land from the Indians. He bought the land from Lord Berkeley in a deal that was supposed to give him title to roughly half of New Jersey. But the deal was rife with legal questions, and the case went to arbitration in England. William Penn was the arbiter, and ruled against Fenwick, leaving him with "only" the one hundred and fifty thousand acres of what today is most of Salem and Cumberland counties. When Fenwick objected, Penn told him to take it easy. "Thy grandchildren may be in the other world before what land thou hast allotted will be employed." Penn was right: Salem and Cumberland counties remain wide open, even desolate in spots.

But back to the tree. At last count, the tree stood eighty-eight feet high, and its branches and leaves shade an area that's one-quarter of an acre. The tree's reputation for size and longevity are legend in the worldwide horticulture community: for decades, acorns from the tree were collected each fall and shipped around the world to fill orders by tree-growers and experimenters. The tree today is too old to reproduce, but it has descendants far and near, including the Salem County Centennial Oak, which was planted in 1876.

Across the street is another survivor of a bygone era: the Salem Oak Diner, a classic, all metal-and-formica railroad-car style joint, with a green and pink neon oak leaf sign, just to let you know it's there. Crabcake sandwiches, cheese fries and red birch beer on tap, all with a bird's-eye view of the big tree.

The street that runs perpendicular to the Salem Oak and alongside the Salem Oak Diner is—what else?—Oak Street. Although not at the center of Salem's Historic District, Oak Street has a number of historic and older homes from to Federal to Victorian, in different stages of restoration and disrepair. In a few short blocks you can see ghostly mansions, run down by neglect and multifamily overuse, and magnificent homes that have been restored to their original state of elegance.

The Salem County Historical Society

Alexander Grant House
79-83 Market Street (Route 45)
Salem
(609) 935-5004

OPEN: Tuesday through Friday: NOON to 4 P.M., and the second Saturday of the month: NOON to 4 P.M.

COST: $3 for adults, 25-cents for children

DIRECTIONS: Take Route 49 east to the center of Salem, make a left on Market Street (Route 45). Alexander Grant House is one block up on left.

The Alexander Grant House is a twenty-two-room brick mansion that is headquarters to the Salem County Historical Society. Built in 1721, the mansion holds all the things you'd expect in a historical house museum: antique furniture—including a chair made in England in 1678—table settings of fine china, grandfather clocks, ornate chests, and a colonial kitchen with a room-wide hearth, which was discovered in 1982 when workers took down a mantel over what they thought was a standard-sized fireplace.

The unexpected is sequestered away in a two-story barn out back. This is the county attic, where the odds, ends and crazy aunts are stored. Indian artifacts, blacksmith tools, saddles, horse-drawn hearses and carriages, pots and pans, golf clubs, shad-harvesting equipment, knives and swords, guns, mounted animal trophies, stuffed ducks, a stuffed bald eagle, a stuffed albino muskrat, a jar of horse teeth—donated by a local veterinarian.

To top it all off is the walking-stick collection of H. J. Heinz, the ketchup and pickle man himself. While the main headquarters and plants were in Pittsburgh, Heinz opened a packing plant in Salem in 1907. A food innovator—he developed tomato ketchup and sweet pickles—and a marketing genius—he had the largest exhibit at the 1893 Chicago World's Fair and

H. J. Heinz walking-stick collection at Salem County Historical Museum.

put up New York City's largest electric sign in 1900, an attention-grabbing forty-foot pickle—Heinz was best known as a good boss. According to "Hoover's Handbook of Business," Heinz's Pittsburgh plants were called the "utopia for working men," and included a swimming pool, an indoor gym, and a hospital. In a time when industrial labor was beginning to flex its muscles against exploitative owners and management, there was never a strike at any Heinz plant. Heinz was also instrumental in lobbying for the Pure Food Act of 1906, a law that his fellow food-producing magnates campaigned bitterly against.

Heinz's penchant for walking sticks was well-known among his friends, and probably every salesman who visited him. Anytime someone would travel to Europe or more exotic places abroad, they knew what to bring back for H. J. Heinz.

H. J. Heinz must have been a frequent visitor to his Salem plant, and, as another example of his all-around good-guy demeanor, he gave his beloved walking-stick collection to the plant manager there as a gift as he neared the end of his life. Heinz died in 1919, and the walking-stick collection was donated to the county historical society in the early 1930s.

At one time, there were three hundred canes in the collection, but the historical society sold off about a hundred and twenty for five dollars apiece in the 1930s to raise funds to restore the Hancock House (visited later in this chapter). The Heinz plant closed in 1977, and the walking-stick collection, that at one time was a main attraction at the Alexander Grant House, is now stored unceremoniously in a barrel in the barn. Despite it's depleted number, the collection still offers up some good examples of carving art and eccentricity. There are a number of carved birds with glass eyes; a balled-up snake; a couple of deer paw handles, some carved, some the real thing; busts of Victorian gentlemen, one looks very much like Ulysses S. Grant; a few hands, a foot, and more than a few skulls, human and animal. One bird head has a long beak with three holes in it.

Push the button on top of the cranium, and three frogs jump out of the holes. Pretty neat.

The Heinz walking-stick collection, worth the trip to Salem in itself, isn't the only oddball attraction at the historical society. The John Jones Law Office, near the barn, is a free-standing turret, a one-room office no bigger than a well with brick walls. The law office was built on what today is Broadway in 1735, then moved to Market Street. In 1967 it was slated for demolition as the county planned to build a new courthouse. It was saved by the historical society and moved into the backyard of the Grant House.

The Hancock House State Historic Site

Salem-Hancocks Bridge Road
Lower Alloways Creek Township

OPEN: The museum inside the house is temporarily closed. Funds are being raised by a private, concerned-citizens group to re-open the home, which is under state auspices. For more information, call the Fort Mott historian at (609) 935-3218.

COST: Unknown

DIRECTIONS: Take Route 49 east into Salem City, make a right onto York Street (which becomes Salem-Hancocks Bridge Road, Route 658), and head out about 6 miles.

One of the most barbaric incidents of the Revolutionary War happened just south of Salem at the home of Judge William Hancock. In the early morning hours of March 21, 1778, a force of about three hundred Hessians and Tories, under the leadership of top British marauder Major John Simcoe, attacked and killed thirty Revolutionists, many of whom were sleeping. The dead men were locals, and the massacre left the Salem area in mourning, and the rest of the new nation outraged.

It was an unlikely spot for such violence. First, the area, like today, was sparsely populated. Second, it held no major strategic importance other than its being mostly farmland and could help supply both sides with rations, which made Salem no different than the rest of the surrounding areas of New Jersey, Pennsylvania, and Delaware. Third, the area had the usual mix of Revolutionists and British sympathizers and Tories, no more or less a volatile mix than any other place in New Jersey, which was fairly divided from top to bottom.

The trouble began a month earlier when Gen. Anthony Wayne came to Salem looking for cattle to drive back to Valley Forge, where the Continental Army was dug in for the winter. Many local farmers drove their livestock into the woods and swamps, patriotism being a lower priority than feeding their own families.

Wayne found enough of them to make his cattle-drive a success and brought about one hundred and fifty head back to Valley Forge, crossing the river near Trenton.

The British decided to punish the Salem militia and other American sympathizers in the area. Colonel John Mawhood and Major John Simcoe, leaders of a force of expert pillagers who had ransacked homes throughout New Jersey, were dispatched to the area. Simcoe's Raiders, a group of hardened Tories, British thugs and Hessian henchmen, picked up a few Salem Tories along the way to bring their number to about three hundred.

The first group of Salem militiamen to meet the oncoming British was a small detachment at Quinton's Bridge. Seven Salem men were killed in brief, but intense, combat on March 18. (Quinton's Bridge today is on Route 49 just west of Salem in the town of Quinton. A blue historical sign marks the spot, and tells the story. The bridge, which spans Alloways Creek, is easy to miss. Best landmark is Butch's Paint on Wheels autobody shop, which is right next to the bridge, on the west side. On the east side is Smick's Lumber and Hardware.)

The British moved on to Hancock's Bridge. A group of thirty

Salem militiamen had captured the home of Judge William Hancock, a British Loyalist who fled his home when the Americans moved in, but returned shortly before the attack.

In the early morning hours of March 21, Simcoe's Raiders crept into the tiny town of Hancock's Bridge looking for the judge's house, which they knew was inhabited by Salem militiamen. At 4 A.M., while the thirty militiamen and Hancock slept inside, they struck, methodically and silently overpowering and bayoneting the two sentries. They moved through the house, using bayonets on the sleeping militiamen, who were mostly teen-aged boys and middle-aged men. The men who were not killed in the first moments of the attack were trapped and had no place to go but up. They fled the attack, chased by the British, where a few more were stabbed. Eight men, including Hancock, were stabbed and bled to death. Another ten or so were badly wounded.

Legend has it that the bloodstains remained on the attic floorboards for decades to remind everyone of the massacre. The house was also said to be haunted, with ghosts from both sides re-enacting the massacre on full-moon nights.

Whatever. The fact is, the incident is remembered today and the house endures. In fact, the exterior of the home is in pretty good shape, especially the zig-zagging brick patterns on the side walls. The brick work on the side opposite the main road is an example of a common decorating feature of the day: the owner's initials and the year the home was built are stated in large brick numbers and letters, worked into the brick pattern of the wall. At the Hancock House, the information is arranged in a pyramid: a big H for Hancock is laid in just below the roof peak; underneath is a w for William, the father of the William Hancock killed in the blood-letting, and an s, presumably for his wife Sarah; below the w and s, are the numbers 1734, the year the home went up.

BIBLIOGRAPHY

Beck, Henry Charlton. *Jersey Genesis.* New Brunswick, N.J.: Rutgers
    University Press, 1963.

Burton, Hal. *The Morro Castle: Tragedy at Sea.* New York: Viking
    Press, 1973.

Cunningham, John T. *The New Jersey Shore.* New Brunswick, N.J.:
    Rutgers University Press, 1958, 4th edition 1995.

———. *This Is New Jersey.* New Brunswick, N.J.: Rutgers Univer-
    sity Press, 1953.

Di Ionno, Mark. "Sea Worthy and Worth Seeing: The New Jersey
    Coastal Heritage Trail," *The Star-Ledger*, Newark, N.J. Sunday,
    July 3, 1993.

Fleming, Thomas. "New Jersey, A history." W.W. Norton, New
    York, 1977.

Kraft, Bayard Randolph. *Under Barnegat's Beam.* New York:
    Appleton, Parsons & Co., 1960.

McMahon, William. *Historic South Jersey Towns.* Atlantic City, N.J.:
    Press Publishing Company, 1964.

New Jersey Coastal Heritage Trail: Resource Inventory Summary, Washing-
    ton, D.C.: U.S. Department of the Interior, National Park
    Service, 1993.

Pierce, Arthur D. *Smugglers' Woods.* New Brunswick, N.J.: Rutgers
    University Press, 1960.

Roberts, Russell and Youmans, Rich. *Down the Jersey Shore.* New
       Brunswick, N.J.: Rutgers University Press, 1993.

Santelli, Robert. *Guide to the Jersey Shore.* Old Saybrook, Conn.: Globe
       Pequot Press, 1986.

Seabold, Kimberly R. and Leach, Sara Amy. *Historic Themes and
       Resources within the New Jersey Coastal Heritage Trail.* Washington
       D.C.: U.S. Department of the Interior, National Park Service,
       1990.

Van Deventer, Fred. *Cruising New Jersey Tidewater.* New Brunswick,
       N.J.: Rutgers University Press, 1964.

Wilson, Harold F. *The Story of the Jersey Shore.* Princeton, N.J.: D.
       Van Nostrand, 1964.

The WPA Guide to New Jersey. New York: Viking Press, 1939.
       Reprinted by Rutgers University Press, New Brunswick, N.J.,
       1986.

INDEX